FUN Learning damentals

3-6
STARTING SCHOOL

by Colin Rose and Gordon Dryden

First published in the UK in 2001 by Big Fish.
Distributed by Sterling Publishing Company Inc.,
387, Park Avenue South, New York, N.Y. 100016.
Distributed in Canada by Sterling Publishing,
c/o Canadian Manda group, One Atlantic Avenue,
Suite 105, Toronto, Ontario, Canada M6K 3E7.

ISBN: 0-8069-7523-7

British Library Cataloguing in Publication Data
CIP data for this book is available from the British Library

Creative Director:Val Pidgeon
Publishing Director: Chester Fisher

Art Direction and Design: Tessa Barwick
Project Manager: Alex Edmonds
Editor: Jenny Siklós
Indexer: Caroline Hamilton

Photography: Chris Fairclough
Illustration: Kelly Waldek
Production: Kiki Aylward

Printed in Italy

The Authors

Colin Rose

Colin Rose is one of the world's foremost experts on learning. He is the inspiration behind FUNdamentals, and its co-author. He is best known as the man who took the principles of Accelerated Learning out of the theoretical realm of university research and introduced them to the public at large. Founder and Chairman of Accelerated Learning Systems Ltd, he is a consultant to many corporations and universities and in demand as a speaker on learning and education at international conferences and symposiums.

He is also a member of the initial steering committee of the UK's Campaign for Learning. This is an initiative of the Royal Society for the Encouragement of Arts, Manufacturers & Commerce, supported by the British Government and Industry. The campaign will run until 2001. A father of four, Colin lives in Buckinghamshire with his wife Joanna and two youngest children, Alexander and Catherine.

Gordon Dryden

Gordon Dryden is an international writer, researcher, broadcaster, and television producer. He is co-author of The Learning Revolution which has become a top-selling book in countries as diverse as Sweden and New Zealand. His television credits include an extensive period as executive producer of the six-part television series Where To Now? which explored the links between parent education, early childhood development, and later achievement.

An award-winning newspaper and broadcasting journalist, he now lists his occupation as "simplifier." While he spent almost 18 months in England adding to his earlier research to produce this educational program, his home base is normally Auckland, New Zealand, where he lives with his wife of almost 40 years, Margaret. They have a grown up family of four and three grandchildren.

CONTENTS

CREATIVITY

THINKING SKILLS

MUSIC

SCIENCE AND NATURE

MEMORY

SELF ESTEEM

VALUES

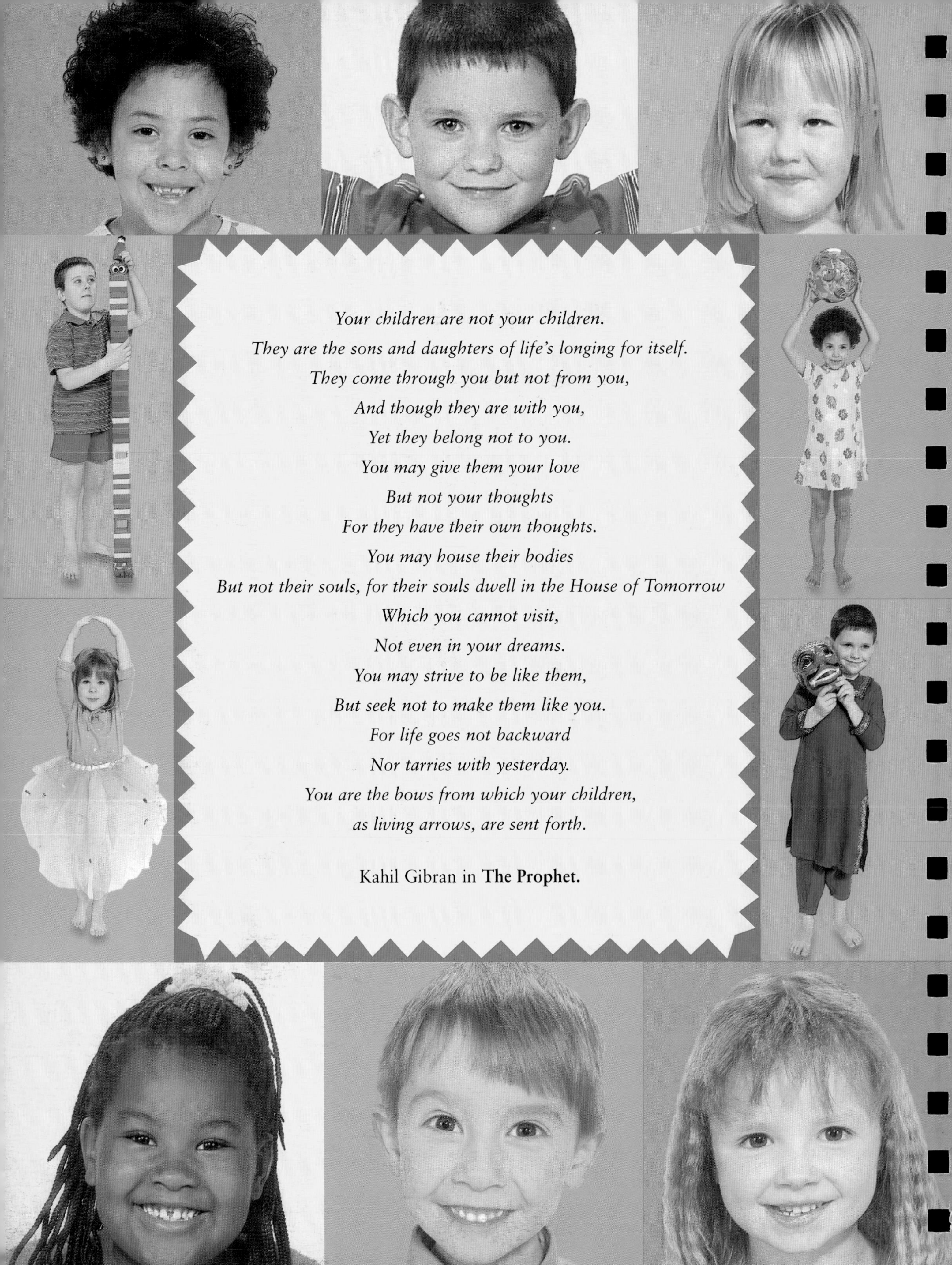

Your children are not your children.
They are the sons and daughters of life's longing for itself.
They come through you but not from you,
And though they are with you,
Yet they belong not to you.
You may give them your love
But not your thoughts
For they have their own thoughts.
You may house their bodies
But not their souls, for their souls dwell in the House of Tomorrow
Which you cannot visit,
Not even in your dreams.
You may strive to be like them,
But seek not to make them like you.
For life goes not backward
Nor tarries with yesterday.
You are the bows from which your children,
as living arrows, are sent forth.

Kahil Gibran in **The Prophet.**

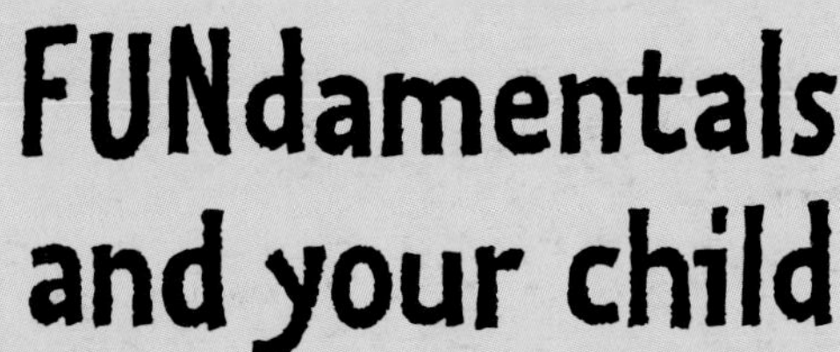

"Children can learn almost anything if they are dancing, tasting, touching, hearing, seeing, and feeling information."

Jean Houston

21st century children

Your child will grow up in the 21st century. *She will live in a world of even faster change and complexity than you and I have experienced: a world that will reward the ability to adapt quickly, to think logically, and to be innovative.

It will be a world that will require self-reliance, and where many of the skills and knowledge that your child will require will be self-taught through new media, such as CD-ROM, the Internet, and Interactive Television.

Yet, despite society's constant emphasis on the technological rather than the social, it will still be a world where kindness, honesty, respect for others, cooperation, and the ability to form close, loving relationships will be at the heart of true happiness. Your child will need to be able to face these new challenges, and the best way to tackle them will be with a strong understanding of basic human values. The building blocks of your child's development are formed very early. The foundations of her education, and the habits that she forms, make the difference between her future success and failure. The secret to helping your child with this magic formula is to provide her with a rich, stimulating environment during the first six years of life. Every child needs a learning environment that has been worked out and planned; one that encourages her to develop truly rounded abilities; an environment which challenges her to think, so she becomes self-confident and excited about learning.

We put the highest possible value on the word "rounded." What would be the point, for example, of helping your child to read early or to be very numerate, if she lacked curiosity, creativity, delight in nature, or the ability to share generously, to relate well and cooperate with others? We also put a high value on the word "planned." To work to a plan doesn't mean you lack spontaneity, laughter, or fun. It merely means that you not only have a dream for your child, but you have also thought out how to best achieve that dream. It's a structured, not a haphazard, development.

*Throughout this book we will alternate between he and she.

The pyramid of happiness

We like to visualize a child's early development as a series of foundation stones and building blocks. These need to be put in place, step-by-step, in order to achieve the ultimate goal of happiness. This pyramid structure is the plan on which the FUNdamentals program is based. The underpinning foundations of that pyramid are the love, security, and fun that you provide for your child.

This whole program is based on games and activities. But while they are lots of fun, they all have a developmental purpose. Each game contributes to one or more of the building blocks. There is a big difference between enjoyable, yet "purposeful" play, and activities that merely fill time and keep your child occupied. When you play a game from FUNdamentals, you can be sure it is contributing directly to your child's physical, emotional, or intellectual development. Hence the double emphasis in our name—FUN-damentals.

HAPPINESS

RESPONSIBILITY | SELF-CONTROL AND RESPECT | COURAGE AND HONESTY

SELF- RELIANCE | COOPERATION AND LOVE | PERSISTENCE AND POSITIVITY

CREATIVITY AND CURIOSITY | LOGIC AND THINKING | LISTENING AND MUSICAL SKILLS | MEMORY AND CONCENTRATION

RICH SPEAKING VOCABULARY | READING | WRITING | MATHEMATICS

BRAIN CAPACITY | FIVE ACUTE SENSES | SEVEN FULL INTELLIGENCES | SELF-ESTEEM | PHYSICAL SKILLS AND HEALTH

LOVE AND SECURITY | FUN

Turning potential into actual intelligence

You'll sometimes hear the argument that pre-school children shouldn't, for example, learn to read; they should be joyfully exploring nature. This misses the point—they can do both. FUNdamentals is built on the conviction that a properly designed word game can be just as much fun as making mud pies. Children need a whole range of activities to bring out their potential.

Brain building: your child is born with more than enough brain cells to be highly successful. More than 100 billion! It's not the number of brain cells that determines usable intelligence, it's the number of connections that are made between those brain cells.

These connections are formed by the experiences and thoughts that you give to your child through the rich, stimulating environment you provide in the early years.

That environment is made up of games, visits, conversations, experiences, activities, and loving attention.

The illustration below says it all. What you do with this program will directly affect your child's brain capacity.

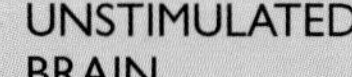

UNSTIMULATED BRAIN		STIMULATED BRAIN	
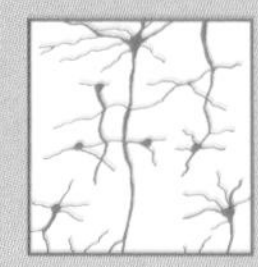	Fewer pathways to develop thought	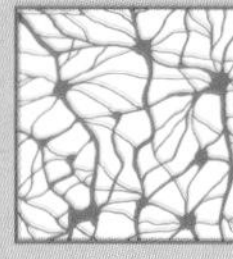	A rich network of pathways to permit complex thinking

Keep it fun!

Throughout FUNdamentals we are careful to stress that you need to create an environment that is sufficiently challenging to produce a feeling of achievement—but never so challenging as to be overwhelming. It's a delicate but vital balance. Over-ambitious parents fail because, instead of support and encouragement, they provide a hot-house environment and pressure. The unshakeable rule is: if your child is not enjoying it, stop immediately.

It's also vital to recognize that each child develops at his own pace. Albert Einstein started talking very late and he failed mathematics early in high school. Yet, of course, he went on to become the greatest scientist of his age. Winston Churchill initially talked with a stutter and a lisp. Yet he became one of the 20th century's greatest leaders. Give your child a chance.

The only race your pre-schooler is in is the human race.

The great thing about the FUNdamentals book is that you can take it wherever you go, so inspirational activity ideas will always be at hand. This way you can choose new games and activities that suit the moment.

Never impose an activity on your child; let the game or activity develop naturally.

Try to incorporate several different types of games or activities each day. You might play a reading game, then a music game, then a creativity exercise, then a math game, then a vocabulary game, then a physical activity. It's the variety that's important.

The cards at the back of this pack go hand-in-hand with this book. They will help to build your child's skills gradually and solidly through motivating, natural play.

A rounded child

The central idea of FUNdamentals is to combine fun and laughter with games and activities that promote all-round strengths.

Is your child likely to read early? Yes, because it's fun. Will she really understand counting, adding, subtracting, dividing, and even multiplying by the time she's five or six years old? Yes, because we've made it fun. Will she write before school? Yes. But she'll also develop her early musical, artistic, social, and creative skills, along with a love of learning, memory skills, self-esteem, thoughtfulness, a respect for nature, values ...

No single ability is more important than any other—the goal is all-round ability.

The foundations for the whole range of human talents and abilities are laid down in these all-important first years of life.

What a wonderful, awesome, exhilarating, challenging opportunity that is for us as parents.

We are our children's first and most important teachers.

That's why it's necessary to work to a plan.

And that's the justification for the time, commitment, and love that this program needs you to offer your child. The years in which your child will prefer to be with you, rather than playing with her friends, are all too short. So live them together to the full. The activities and games you play today will build more than ability, they will build bonds and loving memories.

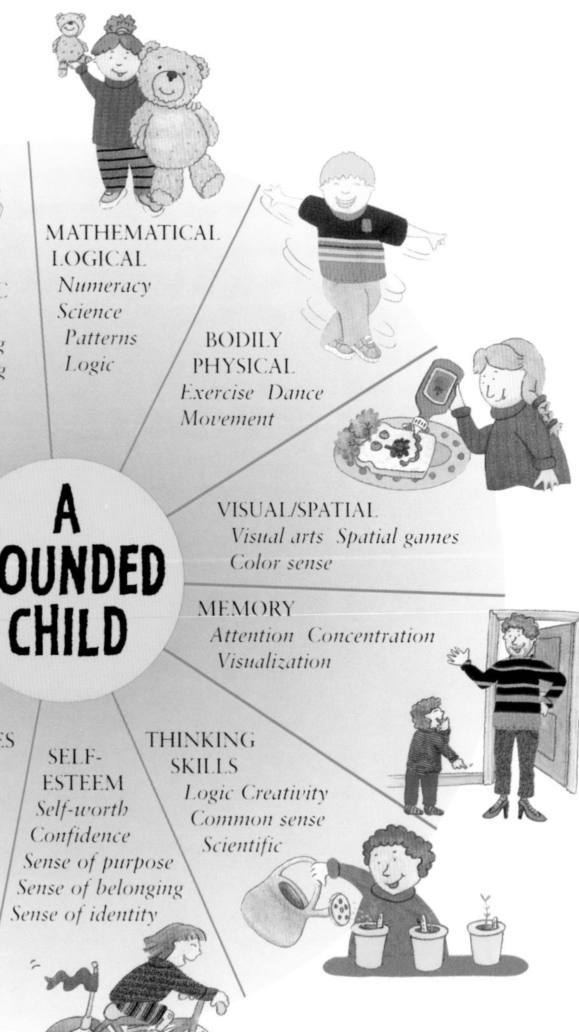

Making the most of the activities

It's not just the activities and games you play with your child that develop her. The way you play them makes a big difference. The following ten principles will help you to help your child become an independent-minded, thoughtful, self-motivated, 21st century child.

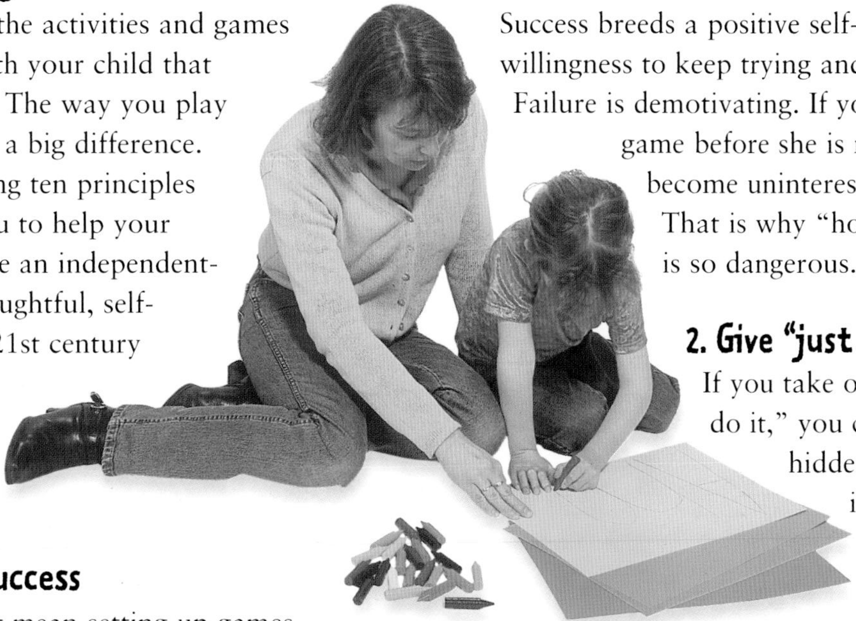

1. Ensure success

That doesn't mean setting up games and activities which are too easy. It means you should gradually extend the challenges—challenges she can solve, often on her own, with a bit of thought and effort.

If your child can remember three objects in a memory game, but not four, play the game again using three things, until she is ready to try four.

If she's getting restless or inattentive, she's becoming overloaded—stop, or lower the level of difficulty. Your aim is for her to do a little bit more each time, with regular encouragement: "Lena, you've read four new words today, that's better than before. Well done."

Success breeds a positive self-image and a willingness to keep trying and learning.

Failure is demotivating. If you try to play a game before she is ready, she may become uninterested in learning. That is why "hot-housing" is so dangerous.

2. Give "just enough" help

If you take over, saying, "Let me do it," you convey a strong hidden message that she is not competent. On the other hand, never leave her struggling.

Give as much help as she needs to succeed—and no more. It's an important and delicate balance. Be sensitive. Help her break a big task down into small steps—and then stand back. This builds self-confidence and independence.

It's also very important to constantly emphasize that mistakes are part of learning. Use phrases like: "We all learn from mistakes. What can we learn from this?" and, "Well, that didn't work out quite right, let's see why." This helps your child to see that mistakes are not the end of the world.

3. Practice "show and tell"

Too much verbal instruction swamps and confuses children. Equally, to demonstrate something without an explanation doesn't work either—they often misunderstand the steps involved. So show and tell her at the same time, then let her experiment for herself. She learns most, not when you are her teacher, but when you are her fellow-learner and guide.

4. Give her time to work it out herself

Avoid rushing in to help. If you ask her a question, leave a long enough pause for her to give you a well-thought-out answer.

Encourage her to think things through herself. Let her correct her own efforts if possible. Help her to put her thoughts into her own words. Use expressions like: "What do you think?" regularly and, "Let's think about this a bit more."

5. Give encouragement rather than praise

If your response is: "Good girl" she will come to want to do things to please you rather than herself. Trying to succeed in order to please herself, however, is self-motivation. Self-motivation lasts and is what she will need in later life. So give encouragement that contains helpful advice like, "Good, you succeeded because you looked carefully" or, "You did well that time because you did it a bit more slowly."

6. Encourage methodical thinking

Think things out aloud yourself. Say, "I wonder why that is?" Then wait for her explanation. If you provide the answers, she will come to assume that answers lie in what adults and teachers think—not in what she thinks. She will wait for an answer, rather than thinking it out for herself. If you prompt her to think for herself, deliberately and methodically, helping with the words she needs, you create self-confidence.

With such support, children of four and five can typically tackle tasks that they may otherwise not tackle until seven or eight. Here are three powerful thinking steps.

Help her see what's important
If, for example, you were doing a jigsaw puzzle together you might say, "Now let's look carefully. What do you think we should do first?" Pause. "Well, let's put the box lid in front of us, so we know what the picture will be like when it's finished. Then let's turn all the pieces face up, and get all the pieces of sky together. That makes the job easier."

Help her take time and plan
"Let's stop and think. Where shall we start? Do you think we should do all the outside edges first? What do you think?" or perhaps, "What about starting at the corners? There's only four of those, so it's a good place to start."
Children are naturally impulsive. Keep using the phrase, "Let's stop and think." Point out that making a plan—and not just rushing in—saves time later.

Encourage her to take care
Children tend to rush, so make sure she concentrates and gives the task her full attention. "Let's take care so we do it right. Let's look carefully. What shape are we looking for?"

7. Avoid rewarding with treats

That's external motivation. The effort disappears when the bribe disappears. Your aim is for internal motivation where the feeling of success in meeting a challenge—a sense of self-mastery —is its own reward. Say, "I bet you're proud that you can do that," rather than, "I'm proud of you." She should want to please herself with her own efforts, rather than please you.

8. Take your lead from his interests

Suggest games, provide options, but let him choose what he wants to do.

9. Encourage curiosity

Encourage him to look around at everything—to wonder, to ask why, how, what? You do this best by being curious and questioning as well.

10. Avoid comparison with other children

Children progress at quite different rates in many different fields of endeavor. Secondly, people who come to compare themselves with others set themselves up for disappointment. There's always someone richer, brighter, more artistic, or more attractive.

How to use the activities

Now you can progress on to the activities. Shown below is an example of the type of activity that we base our FUNdamentals program on. The **What to do** section explains what the activity is all about and how to do it. Then **How it helps your child to learn** explains the different intelligences and skills that are developed as a result of this activity. The **Special tip** and **And another thing!** boxes give you extra hints and advice on how to further develop related skills and interests. Work through these activities at your leisure. Enjoy them with your child and think of them not just as an educational tool, but also as a chance to spend quality time with your child.

World traveler

What to do

Add an inflatable globe to the bath. Show him where he lives, and ask where he would like to travel to. Or ask him to close his eyes as you spin the globe, and point to a spot when it stops. Then tell him some facts about his destination, such as, "That's the Arctic. Polar bears live there. It's really cold."

How it helps your child to learn

This activity builds an understanding of the world, and other people and countries—giving him a basic grasp of geography in a few months.

Special tip

You only need elementary facts—the Pacific is the largest ocean, China has the most people, Egypt makes cotton, etc.

And another thing!

If he is enthusiastic about this activity, try introducing him to books on geography or any other subject that he has shown interest in.

Just for dads!

FUNdamentals is for both parents. But here are some important points for dads that, in my experience as an educationalist, I have known them to not pick up on.

Play mental as well as physical games

Girls outperform boys during the first ten years of school. One reason is that dads tend to play more rough-and-tumble games with sons than with daughters. So girls have more chances to experience pre-school activities that involve sitting down, quiet concentration, and persistence—and that prepares them better for school. Don't stop the rough-and-tumble games with either your son or daughter. But be sure to also play thinking games, memory games—and to do some reading, too.

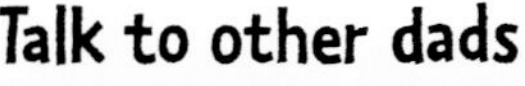

Talk to other dads

Being a dad is probably the most important job you'll ever have, so talk to other fathers and get advice. Talk over problems and ideas. In general, men create far fewer opportunities to talk over personal and parenting issues than women. So take the initiative, and talk about your children.

Become a good listener

Good listening is an art. Children, like adults, don't always say what they really mean. They often have worries, concerns, doubts, and emotions that they don't know how, or hesitate to express. Become sensitive to your child. Use phrases like: "Let me see if I really understand how you feel." "Is this what you mean?" "How can I help?" Sons, as well as daughters, need to be able to express concerns and feelings openly.

Show that your child is your first priority

When you get home, leave your work concerns behind. It isn't easy, but enter the door ready to give her time, love, and your full attention. Your child's early development will take a lot of your time. It may mean giving something up. There's no way around that. She needs you to play, guide, support, love, laugh, and listen—wholeheartedly. If time is limited, take encouragement from child experts Tizzard and Hughes: "It may be that one episode of real concentration on a child each day, or one question seriously answered, is as valuable as hours of less focused attention."

Start with love and security

Love is an active verb

Of course you tell your child each day how much you love her, but demonstrate it as well. That way she can see for herself how love is shown by little acts of kindness. She can then create such moments of thoughtfulness for the people she loves in later life.

Write "love you" notes every now and then

Write special notes and make them a surprise. Slip them in her pocket, under pillows, or stick them on the refrigerator, or on her door. Encourage your child to write them, too. If she can't read, read them to her—it will make her to want to read.

Children need physical security

That means the physical contact of hugging. Say you need a hug when you feel depressed, and let her know it's made you feel better.

Mail her something small

About once a month, mail her a crayon, a coloring book, or a badge. Children love to see their name on letters and it starts the day nicely.

If you have to be away, try out these ideas:

Leave a photograph of yourself in her bedroom with a message saying, "I love you," or a surprise note that your partner can put on the breakfast plate the first day. Or put separate messages in envelopes marked Monday, Tuesday, and so on, to be put on the breakfast table each day.

Always remember to bring back something from your trip—a miniature shampoo bottle, a hotel pen, or an airline souvenir can be an exciting gift.

Let her choose photos for the family album

Why not give her the spare photos to make up her own album?

Try to give your child undivided attention

When you are with her, clear your head of home or work problems and focus on her alone. Pay close attention to what she is saying, so that she feels that what she's saying is important.

Mark special occasions

The day she first rode a bicycle unaided, a particularly impressive effort at writing, the day she could read 100 words, or draw a house. Put them in her own Book of Me.

Try and bring back a memento of each major visit, trip, day out, or holiday together—also for the Book of Me. It provides lots to talk about and remember as you look at them later.

"Thank you" notes

When your child has done something especially helpful, write out a blank postcard with a simple "thank you" such as, "Thank you for looking after Catherine for me, that really helped." Each of these activities may be small in itself, but each helps your child absorb an important lesson: that love needs to be nurtured actively: it must be shown—as well as felt.

The seven intelligences

Brain research has forever shattered the myth of fixed intelligence. We are not born with a single fixed "intelligence quotient" or IQ. Each of us has the potential to develop at least seven different "intelligences." They are:

- *Linguistic intelligence—* The ability to read, speak, and write well—highly developed in people such as Churchill, Kennedy, Shakespeare, and Jane Austen.
- *Mathematical-logical intelligence—* The ability to reason, calculate, and think logically—highly developed in economists, scientists, engineers, lawyers, and accountants.
- *Visual-spatial intelligence—*The ability to paint, draw, take imaginative photographs, create sculptures, or to visualize three-dimensional space. Highly developed in navigators and also in artists such as Picasso and Michelangelo.
- *Musical intelligence—*The ability to compose songs, sing, play musical instruments, create poetry, use rhyme and rhythm.

- *Interpersonal (or "social") intelligence —* The ability to relate to others—strong in sales people, teachers, and natural leaders.
- *Intrapersonal (or "reflective") intelligence—* The ability to focus on inner feelings, draw conclusions from experiences, and make plans.
- *Bodily-physical intelligence—* The ability to use one's hands or body—strong in gymnasts, dancers, craftsmen, and athletes.

To the above seven intelligences Dr Howard Gardner has recently added an eighth:

- *Naturalist intelligence —* The ability to understand and be in tune with nature.

Five Acute Senses

"To learn anything fast and effectively, you have to see it, hear it, and feel it."

Tony Stockwell in Accelerated Learning in Theory and Practice.

Building five acute senses

Throughout his life, your child will take in new information through his senses. Like you, your child has five main pathways into his brain. He learns by what he sees, hears, touches, tastes, and smells. The more you help him develop the five acute senses, the better the pathways (on which all his future learning is based) will be laid.

From his very first days, he is developing the parts of his brain that deal with vision, smell, and hearing. Then, as he develops other brain pathways in sequence, he learns to talk, sing, draw, read, write, think, and create.

For the first eight years of life, and especially the first four, a child has a truly absorbent mind. He simply soaks up experiences. Take advantage of this by providing as many sensory experiences as possible. For example, while he is still a baby, you should add as many opportunities to crawl as possible. Many experts feel that the action of crawling—where the child uses all four limbs in a cross pattern sequence—is an important way to strengthen the pathways that link both sides of the brain.

Healthy body, healthy mind

Different parts of the brain control different parts of the body. The more movement and touching experience a youngster gets in the first few years of life, the more thorough the base for all-round education later. Those physical and tactile experiences actually grow new branches on the billions of active cells that make up the human brain.

Jerome Hartigan, who has a Masters degree in physical education says: "If children learn to love physical exercise, that physical activity will greatly increase their "academic" learning skills. Without "motor" learning, the brain simply will not develop." Hartigan says specific movement patterns "wire up" the brain. So, certain walking, running, and clapping exercises lead to coordinated counting, which in turn leads to arithmetic; following patterns of physical movement leads to making patterns on paper, which in turn leads to writing—and so on.

The activity cards at the back of the book include lots of appropriate ideas. The common sense approach is to create a variety of activities. Hold your child in your arms, dance to music, turn her upside-down, roll her over, and spin her in both directions. Hartigan recommends exercises that involve grasping and stretching: for example, swinging on safe "jungle gyms" or "monkey bars." Learn plenty of action songs and rhymes that involve marching, jumping, and hopping. "Get your children to do combinations of things they can remember," says Hartigan. "Get them to throw a ball first into a red hoop, then a blue one, then a green. Or select three different objects and say, 'Can you run around the tree, jump over that little rock, and crawl under the table?' " In this way, memory is developed while getting healthy exercise and having fun.

Moving into the top 10 percent

Dr. Lyelle Palmer is Professor of Education at Winona State University in Minnesota. He has completed extensive studies with five-year-olds who attended a gymnasium daily as a key part of early schooling. They carried out a simple series of routines: spinning, jumping rope, balancing, somersaulting, climbing, rolling, and walking on balance beams.

In the playground, they swung on low monkey bars, climbed, roller-skated, performed somersaults, and flips. In class, they played with a wide range of games designed to stimulate their sight, hearing, and touch. At the end of each year, the children took a test to measure whether they had developed enough to start first-grade schooling.

Nearly all passed the tests in the top 10 percent for the state—and most were in the top five percent. Nearly all came from low income backgrounds.

Dr. Palmer, also a former president of the International Alliance for Learning, stresses that the children were not just walking, running, and skipping (normal "motor" activities.) "The stimulation activities we recommend," he says, "are specifically designed to activate the areas of the brain we know will promote their sense of sight, touch, and hearing—as well as their ability to take in knowledge." We have included many of these activities in this book.

Dr. Palmer's exercise recommendations

Dr. Lyelle Palmer recommends a regular sequence of physical activities which includes:

- log rolls
- ball catch
- forward rolls
- helicopter spins
- hanging upside-down

He also states that the slow, controlled movements of T'ai Chi are very effective in developing body control.

He sounds a warning note, however, "We are heading for a health and fitness crisis with even young growing children adopting a more sedentary lifestyle."

The helicopter spin

What to do

Get your youngster to stand, with hands outstretched, and spin as fast as possible for 15 seconds. Say, "Stop and close your eyes. Keep your balance. Remain standing." Stand still for 25 seconds until he no longer feels dizzy. Repeat five times, always spinning the same way each day. Repeat daily.

How it helps your child to learn

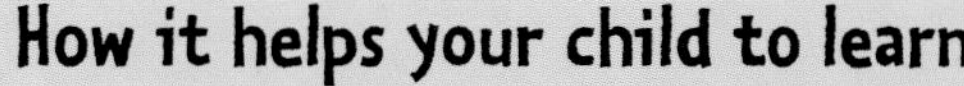

The helicopter spin makes the ear-fluid move rapidly inside the ear mechanism, and this helps grow new, active cells in the part of the brain that develops the sense of balance and the "muscle-memory" needed for writing and reading. Spinning, tumbling, somersaulting, and jungle gym exercises stimulate the vestibular system, the area controlling balance.

Special tip

If your child has difficulty in spinning, stand with him and help by grasping one hand and pulling it quickly to start the spin.

And another thing!

Gymnastic exercise is credited as helping youngsters in the US jump to the top 5 percent in reading and writing tests.

Parts of the body

What to do

Using large sheets of cardboard, trace parts of your child's body: forearm, hands, fingers, etc. Cut around the outlines. Link your "skeleton" together by sewing it with thread or with paper-clips. Now write on the names of the parts of the body: index finger, "funny bone," and Achilles tendon.

Later say you are going to ask him if he likes something (such as cheese.) He must wiggle his toe for "yes" or touch his earlobe for "no." Vary the questions and parts of the body in future games. Then he builds up a complete vocabulary for body parts.

How it helps your child to learn

Physical intelligence at its best: using one's own body as the starting point to explore a subject scientifically.

Special tip

You'll probably find it best to discover and write the name of one body part or bone at a time, with your child choosing which one.

And another thing!

As you learn each part, play the "body part" game as the fancy takes you, "Who's the first to touch their Achilles tendon?"

Exploring taste

What to do

Place a little bit of sugar on one spoon, some salt on another, some lemon juice on another, and some vinegar on a fourth. Blindfold your child and direct her finger to each spoon in turn. Let her touch each ingredient and then place her finger in her mouth and guess what it is. Then get her to say on which part of her tongue she could taste it.

(NB: The front of the tongue records sweet tastes, the side-front salty, the side-back sour, and the back bitter.)

How it helps your child to learn

The more variety that is tasted early, the better a child can appreciate different flavors and textures.

Special tip

Talk about tastes to build vocabulary—crunchy peanut butter, or smooth creamy yogurt with sweet, juicy strawberries.

And another thing!

Taste and smell are closely related. Get your child to hold her nose while tasting anything. Release it and note the difference.

Bouncing to learn

What to do

This game involves physical actions for learning the alphabet, spelling, addition and, later, times tables. All you need is a ball!

Let's take the alphabet. You think of a first name beginning with A, and something to sell, e.g.:

A. My name is Adam and I sell apples.

B. My name is Beth and I sell books.

C. My name is Chris and I sell cauliflowers.

D. My name is David and I sell daffodils.

As you say the words, you bounce the ball.

How it helps your child to learn

This is a great learning aid for more physically orientated children, great also for coordination and memory training.

Special tip

Use the repeat/bounce combination to learn numbers. So, 1 plus 1 is 2 (2 bounces), 2 plus 1 is 3 (3 bounces), etc.

And another thing!

Later you can not only chant the times tables, you can also bounce to it. The extra physical element aids memorization.

Stimulating toys

Especially good are:

- Wooden blocks in squares, oblongs, triangles, half-circles, diagonals, curves, and pillars, that she can build with.
- Simple musical instruments, such as a small xylophone, bells, tambourine, triangle, drum.
- A magnifying glass and a torch.
- A peg board, over which you can stretch elastic bands to make simple geometric shapes.
- Take-apart trucks and toys.
- A playhouse if you can afford it (or make it out of some cardboard boxes.)
- A box full of disposable packaging, yogurt cartons, cardboard cartons, plastic containers, plastic jars, toilet roll tubes, string.
- A giant magnet to experiment with.
- Child-sized kitchen and cleaning equipment: a soft broom, floor mop, small dustpan, a dusting brush, and some other small cleaning brushes.
- A small watering can, vegetable brush, dishcloth, sponge, basket, and small plastic buckets can also be much better investments than expensive toys.

Stimulating visits

Outings stimulate the senses, build vocabulary and help her find out how things work. It's not just zoos, museums, parks, and rivers that have educational value. There's lot's to see, talk about, and explore at:

- Airport, dock, or ferry terminal
- Antiques store
- Market gardens, "Pick Your Own," or your local Post Office sorting room
- Garage sale
- Top of a cathedral or tower
- Farm, or agricultural show
- Recycling center, or junk yard
- Brass rubbing in a church
- Different religious centers from your own neighborhood
- Local newspaper
- Butterfly farm
- Water-works
- Bakery
- Local factory
- Horse-racing stable
- Police station
- Fire station
- Art gallery
- Radio or television station
- Historic village
- A circus or carnival
- Shoe repair store
- Dog training class
- Shopping trip

Special tip

Stores have lots of learning potential. Count the number of jobs you can see. Talk about the skills or training needed to work there.

And another thing!

Some food manufacturers provide interesting leaflets and many encourage factory visits.

Bean bag games

What to do

Make one bean bag for each member of the family by pouring half a cup of uncooked beans into a small bag. Squeeze air out of the bag, and seal with a plastic tie. Put the bag in an old sock, seal it, and trim off any surplus material.

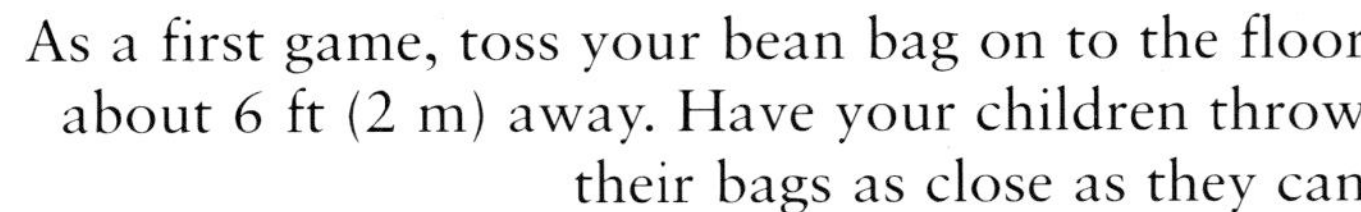

As a first game, toss your bean bag on to the floor about 6 ft (2 m) away. Have your children throw their bags as close as they can to your bag. The closest each time wins.

How it helps your child to learn

Very good for hand-eye coordination.

Special tip

Bean bags are better than balls for many games—try covering obstacle courses with a bag balanced on your head.

And another thing!

As an alternative to the bean bag throw, draw a circle or a line on the floor, and see who can throw into the circle or nearest the line.

Family balancing act

What to do

Get your youngster to try and balance all sorts of things as she moves from one part of your house or garden to another. Get her to balance a feather on one hand or a book, a box, or pack of cards.

Alternatively, get her to walk fast with a book on her head, or lay on her back with her feet in the air balancing various items on the soles of her feet.

How it helps your child to learn

This is good for posture and balance – it also helps set up "muscle memory" in the special part of the brain that records balance.

Special tip

Outside, she might balance long, thin items, such as a broom or a baseball bat on her hands. But teach about safety first.

And another thing!

Juggling is another activity that helps physical coordination. You can start with two soft balls and work up to proper balls.

"Language is the most powerful instrument of human progress."

Maria Montessori in **What You Should Know About Your Child.**

A Rich Speaking Vocabulary

Words let us think, create ideas, and reason. A poor vocabulary leads to a poor level of reasoning. A rich vocabulary, in contrast, leads to higher levels of reasoning and creativity, and skill in communication—skills that are highly valued in later life. It all starts with a love of words. Although there are over 500,000 words in the English language, just 3,000 make up the great majority of the words we use in everyday conversation. About 400 make up 65 percent of the words that a child is likely to come across in children's books. The activities and games in the activity cards will help develop their reading and speaking skills.

Apart from the 3,000 main words that make up our everyday vocabulary, thousands more come from them, using prefixes such as dis-, mis-, re-; and suffixes such as -ed, and -ful.
Once a child has grasped the meaning of these prefixes and suffixes, he's well on his way to unlocking nearly all the secrets of the language's vocabulary.

Talk, talk, talk to him!

To learn to speak the basics of a language before starting school is a fantastic achievement. It is achieved largely through meaningful interaction between you and your child. Speak to him and take time to tell him nursery rhymes, for example. Above all, tell him what is happening when it is happening. The brain stores information in groups of ideas. So when you see a new subject—a dog or a flower—try to build

on your child's existing knowledge by talking about what you see. The more you link ideas together the more she will learn. Later you can talk about what you saw and discuss it again.

Read to your child every single day

Look for children's stories filled with vivid language, and introduce your family to some of the classic literature from quite an early age. But don't force this. Build on your child's interests.

Talk about what you're doing

"I'm going to make dinner now. Do you want to help me? Right, let's scrape some carrots. Here they are. And these are parsnips."
Talk about the different colors and the different textures.
Then as soon as she knows the difference, ask her to bring you some parsnips or carrots.

You can also talk to her when she's dressing: "Now I'm dressing you. Remember: this is your right leg, and this is your left. Which is your left leg? Which is your right?"

Positive encouragement

If she says, "I goed to grandma's," don't tell her that it's wrong. Instead, try: "You went to grandma's yesterday didn't you? And I went, too. Tomorrow we'll both go again."
Nursery rhymes are easy to remember. The rhythm and rhyme in age-old stories—as well new stories such as Dr. Seuss—give children wonderful opportunites for acquiring new vocabulary.

Play word games

As you drive around, play lots of word games and tell silly stories to each other. A good game is to take turns in finding words that start with the same letter: "My grandma's cat eats munchy melon, meatballs, and mouldy mandarins."

Invent stories

One of the best activities of all, however, is regularly making up stories. Start the story, and then take turns adding one sentence at a time to it with your child. You can also write down some of your best stories and read them back to him.

Mastering language naturally

By asking a child about what happened earlier in his day or the day before, you are naturally developing his mastery of the past tense. Ask him to describe what happened in a book or a video. Use photos or mementos to trigger his memories of past trips and add to his own account with even more descriptive words.

By asking what will happen when daddy comes home or when grandma visits, you get him speculating, and, therefore, using the future tense with words like "probably" or "perhaps."

There is no better time to start learning a foreign language than in the pre-school and early years, around 4 or 5 years of age, because children master accents more easily then. Tapes of songs and nursery rhymes in the foreign language help accustom your child to its music, rhythm, and sounds, and add to the fun.

Seek opportunities to introduce new words

Find a natural way to repeat a new word, once it's been explained, in a slightly different context within a few minutes. This reinforces it in your child's mind.

Cooking together can be a great opportunity to introduce new words and ideas.

Color games

What to do

While out walking, take turns seeing who's first to spot something, for example, blue. Start with primary colors: red, yellow, green, and blue.

Ask her to touch as many blue things (or soft, hard, or wooden things) as possible indoors. How many yellow foods can she think of? How many things in the house are white?

Later, start to broaden your child's knowledge by explaining navy blue, khaki, emerald, gold, or cherry. Explain where some of the names come from—such as fruits, precious stones, and metals.

How it helps your child to learn

Color knowledge helps visual discrimination as well as vocabulary (there are tens of thousands of color shades).

Special tip

Describe colors in words that conjure up other senses —chocolate, lime, citrus, lavender, and peach.

And another thing!

For older children, link the color game with sizes—"Who's first to see something green that is bigger than a plant?"

World traveler

What to do

Add an inflatable globe to the bath. Show him where he lives, and ask where he would like to travel to. Or ask him to close his eyes as you spin the globe, and point to a spot when it stops. Then tell him some facts about his destination, such as, "That's the Arctic. Polar bears live there. It's really cold."

How it helps your child to learn

This activity builds an understanding of the world, and other people and countries—giving him a basic grasp of geography in a few months.

Special tip

You only need elementary facts—the Pacific is the largest ocean, China has the most people, Egypt makes cotton, etc.

And another thing!

If he is enthusiastic about this activity, try introducing him to books on geography or any other subject that he has shown an interest in.

'Grandmother's Cat' game

What to do

An old favorite all the family can play. Each person takes a turn, saying something like, "My grandmother's cat eats (or likes) buzzards." The others have to think of other objects that start with the letter B.

Or the game can be played with adjectives, such as, "My grandmother's cat is a happy cat." And the others have to think up other adjectives such as hungry, horrible, or hopeful. Or you can use two words that start the same, "My grandmother's cat likes sizzling sausages."

How it helps your child to learn

Great fun in building word power.

Special tip

This game, and its variations, are ideal for playing in a car or at a party. Take turns suggesting starter words.

Double word games

Children love to learn words that sound like their meaning (onomatopoeic words.) So try to include words like:

babbling	grizzling	plodding
braying	groaning	rapping
buzzing	heckling	ringing
chattering	honking	screaming
cheeping	humming	screeching
chuckling	juddering	sizzling
clanging	jostling	thumping
gasping	meowing	tooting
ghastly	nattering	tinkling

And another thing!

To improve memory, ask each person to remember the previously-added words, "...a furry, fantastic, fun-loving cat."

How many can you name?

What to do

"Naming games" provide hours of fun—and thoughtful learning. Simply choose a category and challenge family members to name as many items as they can that fit into it. Such as:

Things to drink	Vegetables	
Ways of traveling	Farm animals	
Types of sport	Dinosaurs	
Animals that growl	Countries	
Zoo animals	Kitchen tools	
Items of furniture	Breakfast foods	Things that fly
Fruits	Types of metal	Musical instruments
Things that float	Things made of wood	etc, etc.

How it helps your child to learn

Develops memory skills and encourages your child to think in categories.

Special tip

Try to think of some more challenging categories once your child has got the idea of it.

'Simon Says'

What to do

Explain the "rules" of this old-time favorite game. When you preface an action by saying, "Simon Says" he must copy you. But if you suggest an action without saying, "Simon Says" he must not move.

"Simon Says **'Put your hand on your head'**."—then he must copy you.

"**Take your hand down.**"—he must leave it where it is.

How it helps your child to learn

He must not only pay attention, but also stretch his imagination when you say things like, "Simon says: 'Pretend to tread on hot sand,' 'Be excited,' 'Be sad,' 'Shiver with ice down your back.' "

You can also call out sounds instead of actions!

Special tip

A similar game: Say you're going to call out some animals. If you call a bird he must flap his arms. If it's not a bird, he must stay still.

And another thing!

Ask him to freeze in position. Then tell him to melt slowly. Then to return to the "freeze" pose. This builds body awareness and memory skills.

Other people's jobs

What to do

Let your child carry out some garbage. When the garbage truck comes, point out what's happening and talk about the garbageman's job and how we need him. Who pays for the garbageman? When we pay for something at a store where does the money come from? Where do the goods in the store come from?

Talk about what happens when we post a letter.

Your child will become alert to the fact that things don't just happen, they are planned.

How it helps your child to learn

This builds vocabulary, and demonstrates how our society is built on cooperation.

Special tip

Look for other jobs to discuss—bus driver, street repair men, librarian, bank clerk, fireman, or policeman.

And another thing!

How does gas get to the pumps, food to the supermarket, money into the cash machine? Ensure he doesn't take things for granted.

Rhyming words

What to do

Start by saying a word. The next player must say a word that rhymes with it. For example:

play/day/pay/may/stay/hay/
lay/ray/say/way/jay.

Establish a record of the most rhymes and try to beat it. See opposite for more rhymes and two more challenging variations.

Try rhyming sentences, "I saw a bear, comb her hair" or, "I saw a dog, fall off a log" or, "A girl called Sue, got stuck with glue."

Special tip

If she gets stuck, after say, "car," "far," or "jar," try prompting her by saying, "How about the black stuff on the road?" "Oh yes, tar!"

How it helps your child to learn

It's an excellent game to reinforce phonic skills.

Some more words to rhyme with:

sight	toad	pail	make	call
seat	bank	pink	fear	race
sound	rail	rug	care	home

Good double rhymes include:

A pig in a wig, a vet in a jet, a bad lad, a hen with a pen, a bee in a tree, a fish on a dish, etc.

Rhyming colors

Think of a color and an object that rhymes with it. It could be blue shoe, black hat,' green bean, pink sink, violet pilot, gray tray, etc. Once you get beyond the obvious, it builds vocabulary quickly.

Variations on "I Spy"

What to do

This old favorite can be made harder—or easier—with a little imagination. You normally use the beginning letter e.g., "I spy with my little eye something beginning with B (or buh)," but you also can say:

- What color it is
- What it's made from—e.g., wood, plastic, or metal
- What shape it is—e.g., round, oval, or square
- What its purpose is—e.g., something we eat or wear
- What it rhymes with—e.g., bear for chair

How it helps your child to learn

This game is excellent for developing perception of letter-sounds, particularly as you move on to double consonant sounds such as **ch**, **dr**, **cl**, and **br**.

Special tip

A variation for inside the car is: "See who's the first to spot... " which has the added benefit of developing visual curiosity.

And another thing!

"I Spy" can be made a bit harder for older children by covering endings, too—for example, words ending in **t**, **l**, **ed**, **ay**, or **ox**.

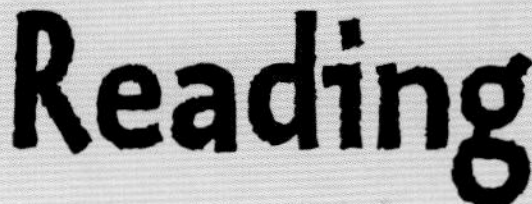

Reading

"Children and parents who read together succeed together."

Peter Young and Colin Tyre in **Teach Your Child to Read.**

Reading – the basics for all ages

Read, read, read!

This is the number one factor in him becoming a successful reader. Here are some simple tips to keep your child actively involved as you read to him.

- Stop every now and then and ask: "What do you think will happen next?" or, "Why is baby bear's bed broken?" Prompt him with, "Because... " In other words, keep him actively involved, instead of just passively listening.
- Run your finger underneath the text occasionally so he reads left to right.
- Re-read a book with simple, large text with your child, rather than to your child. Let him retell the story by looking at the pictures.
- Re-read nursery rhymes and stories and hesitate before a key word so he can supply the word and "read" it at the same time, e.g., "Jack climbed the... (beanstalk)."

Inter-active reading

By stopping regularly during a story, you can recap together what has happened and predict what might happen next. Recapping and predicting are great future comprehension skills. So you can ask:

- What size were the Billy Goats Gruff?
- Why did the Troll let Little Billy Goat Gruff go past?

The keys to reading early are simple

1. The starting point for reading is for your child to recognize the letters of the alphabet. We've created games for that.
2. As we've seen, up to 90 per cent of everyday language is comprised of 3,000 words. If he can read the first 400 of those 3,000 words, he has mastered about 65 per cent of the words he'll find in most of the books he reads.
3. Introduce him to written words in the same sequence as spoken words: nouns first, then verbs, then adjectives and adverbs. And introduce those 400 beginner words in large type. Starting at 2 in (6 cm) and down to 1 in (2.5cm) at about four years old.
4. Play games to introduce him to phonics—the sounds of words—so he can decipher thousands more. Make games of these steps, and most children will be reading confidently before school.

We say this because there is absolutely no difference between the way the brain interprets spoken or written words. If your child HEARS the word DADDY, then nerve pathways from his ears flash that sound to the part of his brain that translates speech. If he SEES the word DADDY, then two nerve pathways from his eyes transmit that message to the part of his brain that interprets vision.

The brain can decode each signal equally well, except for this: in the very early years a child's visual pathways can't pick up a word the size of this type, but they can decode a word this big:

Daddy

Building on these facts, we have created a series of games and inclusions that introduce your child to pre-reading and then reading activities.

Phonic Fun Card sets—Phonics cards look like this. They are also included in this book.

bat	cat	fat	hat
rat	sat	mat	pat
bet	get	met	net
pet	set	wet	yet

Key Word Card Sets—These cards, which look like the following example, are made up of some of the 400 most common words in the language. They can be used to play word Bingo, as well as for testing your child's word knowledge.

at	ate	away	be
before	best	big	black
blue	brown	bus	but
by	call	came	can

The Sentence Game —This is a series of beginning, middle, and ending phrases which can be combined to make a large number of intriguing sentences e.g.:

who	does what
Our family	eats dinner
The big girls	like to swim
My friend	loves to play

All these word card games are designed to be used as a background to the many reading games in FUNdamentals.

In addition, we recommend that you:

- Install a blackboard or whiteboard by your kitchen table or in your child's room.
- Write words regularly on it, or a Magic Word to appear magically every morning.
- Go through a new book and pick out a few new words and then make new cards for them or write them on the blackboard.
- Make her a personalized dictionary of words she wants to read.

Natural readers tend to come from homes where reading is part of everyday life. Homes where people leave notes for each other, keep bulletin boards, telephone notes, write out shopping lists and recipes, read newspapers, and refer to encyclopedias, maps and brochures frequently. When this happens, a child sees that reading is a central and relevant part of life.

In a survey of children who succeed at school, the top predictor of success was the amount of time parents spent talking with their children and the quality of that dialogue.

The second top predictor was that the child should be reading independently of school at an early age.

TV versus books

Why are books so much better than TV? Because TV only uses dialogue. It doesn't need to use descriptive vocabulary for situations and feelings. They are shown.

So a child learning mostly from TV misses out on the vivid descriptive and sensory words which paint pictures when they read stories.

Phonics or whole words?

Forget about the argument as to which method is better: learning by phonics or the so-called "whole-word" or "look and understand" method. It's a pointless argument.

flat
sat
hat
mat
bat
cat

Phonics

chew
yacht
what

Whole-word

The "whole-word" teachers are quite right. And the alphabet-and-phonics teachers are quite right. For a child needs to be able to see words in two quite different ways, for two quite different purposes.

He needs to be able to see the word as a meaningful symbol, so that he can understand it. (That's whole-word.) And he needs to be able to see it as an arrangement of sounds, so that he can translate it. (That's phonics.)

Only about half the words in the English language are spelt phonetically. So phonics alone will not provide anyone with the tools to pronounce or read words like cough, through, enough, bought, drought, or even key, sea, or chief.

So whole-word identification is vital. So are phonics.

As soon as children learn to read simple words such as mat, bat, cat, rat, and sat, they should find it easier to recognize flat, spat, and brat. But, of course, a phonic reading method alone does not help them understand what or yacht.

Phonics is about translating language. So when he knows that unsmiling means not smiling, he can work out what unmade or untied must mean.

How to read together

When your child shows he may be ready to read his first book, choose one with big print. Read it yourself first. Then sit beside him and try this sequence of reading together:

1. Give him "the big picture" first: "This is a story about a friendly dinosaur that travels around town looking for a bunch of flowers to take to his mother for her birthday." Getting the big picture or overview first helps all learning.
2. Read the first passage, with plenty of expression, at a normal pace for about one minute—running your finger under the print.
3. Talk about the story, explaining any points, encouraging any questions.
4. Now suggest he reads the same passage with you—again with you running your finger under the words as you read them together.
5. Praise him for his effort, and suggest you read it again. Continue to run your finger under the words, but pause a few times for the child to provide the next word or phrase. If he hesitates or makes a mistake, pause, then supply the correct word and let him carry on.
6. At the end, praise him for reading so well. And the next time you try that section, suggest that you start and he carries on reading, with you using your finger and picking up any words to keep the pace going.

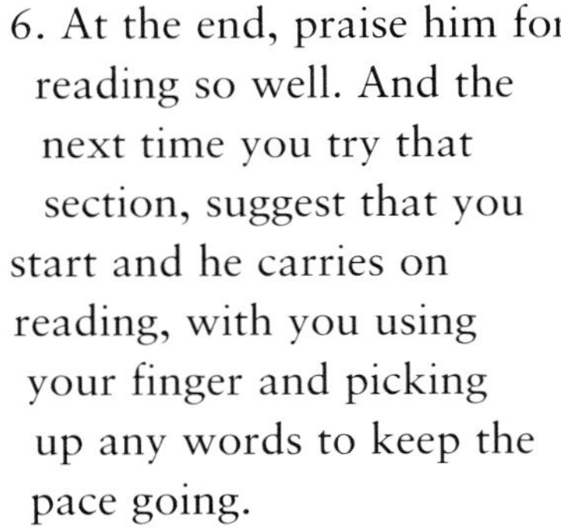

The "pause, prompt, praise" technique is one that also works well when older children help their younger brothers and sisters to read.

From learning to read to reading to learn

One of the key steps to lifelong self-learning is to learn how to use reference sources. When you see a word that you don't understand, look it up together. Talk about what you've found and perhaps write it down with the meaning written under it. Invest in the best children's encyclopedia and world atlas you can afford, and help the family get used to the idea of using it. Above all, get your children used to using the public library. Visit it with them from early on.

Sound alike clap

What to do

Take a FUNdamentals word card and ask him what the initial letter is. Then say you'll say some more words. If one of the words has the same beginning sound as the word on the card, he should clap. If he's right, he keeps the card. How many cards can he collect?

How it helps your child to learn

The starting point in phonics is to recognize beginning letter sounds.

Special tip

This is a good game to play in the car, because you can play it without written words at any time.

And another thing!

Move up to beginning "blends" like **ch**, **pl**, **br** or ending sounds like words ending in **t**.

Alphabet games

What to do

By three or four, most children should know most of the alphabet, but reinforce it by playing alphabet games. Introduce it by saying, "Let's see how many words we know that start the same way as your name. You're Billy, so there's bee, and birds, and bananas. How many can you think of?" The next day, start with another letter. Also think up alternative names e.g,. "Clever Cathy," "Brave Bob," or "Happy Helen."

How it helps your child to learn

The brain stores information in patterns and through association and links—the greater the links the better the memory.

Special tip

In the supermarket or when driving, choose a letter and see how many words your child can find that begin with that letter.

And another thing!

After spotting words with initial letters, try variations such as last letters or letters in the middle. Car license plates are ideal.

A label a day

What to do

Play "A label a day" with your child. Start with our noun cards. Write a word a day and label everything around her room and around the house.

Preferably get her to suggest what she would want labeled. She will soon move onto longer words such as television, videotape, and electric light. Print the labels neatly, in letters at least 1 in (2.5 cm) high, using a red marker.

How it helps your child to learn

Reading can become as easy as speaking if the words are large enough and related to experience.

Special tip

As the labels mount up, encourage more games, such as, "How many words can you see that begin with **b** or **m**?"

And another thing!

From three, you may write the labels with light pencil strokes, and your child could trace over them with darker colors.

The action word game

What to do

When your child is feeling comfortable reading the first noun cards, introduce her to written verbs—by associating them with actions: "Let me see you **walk** over to Daddy. Can you **crawl** under the table? Can you **hide** from me?" Use some of the verb cards with this program, and make up similar-sized extra words.

How it helps your child to learn

The key principle—it is much easier for a child to learn to speak, read, and write if he can associate words with actions—particularly with actions that involve himself.

Special tip

As with nouns, introduce only a few verb cards at a time. Play the game for only a few minutes at a time, so it stays fun.

And another thing!

Later, take three cards and say, "This card says 'hop,' this says 'walk,' and this says 'run.' Can you point to the card that says 'hop'?" Keep it fun.

The 3-step teaching process

What you do

Whenever you're introducing new words (or new objects) to a child, try the three-step teaching process:

Try it with three word cards, for instance: "bear," "lion," and "bird." Point to each card in turn as you pronounce the word.

Next ask her to point to the one that says "lion."

And finally point to another card and ask: "What word does that say?"

How it helps your child to learn

She is not just building memory for specific words, she is seeing the differences in the appearance of words.

Step 1	Show the child the words (or letters) and tell her, very specifically, what they are.
Step 2	Ask her to point to the one that says/is...
Step 3	Now you point to another word (or object) without naming it, and ask her to tell you what it is.

Special tip

Show her three objects e.g., "This is a violin, this is a guitar, this is a tuba." "Which is the violin?" Point to the guitar. "Which one is that?"

And another thing!

This sounds very simple, but it is one of the most sensible ways to get a child to quickly absorb three words (or three pieces of information.)

Phonic Snap

What to do

Divide some phonic cards, face-down into roughly equal piles for each player. Just like ordinary Snap, each person then takes a card from the top of his pile and plays it, in turn, face-up, to make a pile in front of him.

When two rhyming cards appear in sequence, the first player to say "Snap" and place his hand on the pile, wins all the cards. Play until the winner has all the cards.

How it helps your child to learn

Phonics is an essential key to reading. Draw his attention to the fact that it's the **endings** of the words that rhyme.

Special tip

An even simpler introduction is to play so you "snap" when the beginning letter is the same e.g., ball and bed.

And another thing!

When you run out of phonics cards from this book, make your own!

Magic Blackboard

What to do

A strongly recommended reading tool is a blackboard —or whiteboard. Use it to write on and learn:

- A new word daily.
- A word that occurred in yesterday's story.
- A word chosen by your child.
- Phonic ladders e.g., hat, cat, bat, rat, sat.
- A book title.
- Pets and family names.

How it helps your child to learn

Remember: Even a two-year-old can easily read words, AS LONG AS THE LETTERS ARE BIG ENOUGH.

Special tip

Make it a game—treat the words as special and let them appear "like magic."

And another thing!

It helps the magic if the words are already on the board when he comes down in the morning.

Phonic ladders

What to do

You can play more phonics on your white-or black-board. When she's mastered the simpler series—like hat, bat, rat, move up to two-letter blends—as in the illustration.

It's not obvious to a child why **boat** is not pronounced bo-at. Here is a useful rhyme to explain that it is normally the **first** vowel of a double vowel that decides the pronunciation. "When two vowels go out walking, the first vowel does the talking." (Demonstrate it with words like: **tail, fear, sail.**)

Special tip

You can play Starter Snap with phonic word cards. Any two words beginning with the same two letter "blend" e.g., brain and bright, would match.

How it helps your child to learn

A child is launched into reading when she can see into the structure of words. That's what phonics achieves.

big
rig
wig
pig

How high can you climb?

train	boat	bank
brain	coat	sank
drain	goat	drank
strain	float	frank
plain	stoat	crank

When you feel she's mastered the simple concepts, introduce some two-letter blends based on phonics: words that include **ai, ee, sw, ou, tr, sp, sl,** and **ng.** Make up rhyming words together on your whiteboard.

Key Word Bingo

What to do

Make a Bingo board, or use the grids at the back of this book and then make lots of words to go with the board. Pull the words out of a box one at a time. The caller reads the word clearly, twice. If the word is on your Bingo card, cover it up with a counter or coin. The first player to cover a complete line across, down, or diagonally wins.

How it helps your child to learn

The game of Bingo turns whole word recognition into a fun learning experience.

A Bingo Card

after	any	be	best	but
car	don't	fat	funny	going
got	he	him	in	let
me	not	or	ran	saw
six	that	this	walk	with

Special tip

Lay the Bingo cards out alphabetically, from left to right, to make it easier to find words—and to give left to right reading experience.

And another thing!

Let your child color the cards to add color sense to the other lessons he's learning.

Why? Because...

What to do

Ensure your child remains actively involved in his favorite stories by asking questions like: "Why did the little pig's house fall down?" "Why should Goldilocks be scared of the three bears?" "How do you think Snow White felt?"

How it helps your child to learn

It ensures your child is listening for meaning. Successful learners need to be able to find answers to things that make them wonder. They need to be able to think up and ask questions. Encouraging this in a relaxed story-telling situation is an excellent start.

Special tip

For younger children, start with books that have detailed pictures so you can encourage the child to find visual answers to your questions.

And another thing!

If a young child has difficulty answering questions, lead in with some possible answers yourself: "I wonder if he's..."

Shopping for reading

What to do

Whenever you take your child out, turn it into a reading experience. Read the signs along the way, the menu in a restaurant, labels on your purchases, signs at the Post Office, labels on ice-cream cartons. Make it fun, e.g., "See if you can spot the vanilla ice-cream."

Make a shopping list of 2-3 items and ask her to look for them in the supermarket.

How it helps your child to learn

The more you can associate reading with fun experiences, the more your child will connect reading with fun.

Special tip

Keep a good selection of packaging and wrappers. They help her associate words with physical things.

And another thing!

Get your child to point out familiar signs as you're travelling: "Which is the Post Office? Where's the sign that says Savings Bank?"

His special reading box

What to do

If your child shows interest in special words or subjects—such as dinosaurs, animals, or flowers—write each favorite word boldly on a separate card. Write with a bold felt-tip marker, in lower-case letters at least 1 in (2.5 cm) high.

Get your child to store his words in a favorite container. Then review his favorites daily, and let him tell you what each says.

How it helps your child to learn

The best learning is based on personal interests.

dinosaur

crocus

Special tip

Don't be worried if the words seem too complex. Children get great delight from remembering big words.

And another thing!

Food words are great for sight cards, as you can use them to talk about smells and tastes, thus building on more than one sense.

First sentence games

What to do

When your youngster is reading individual words well, introduce him to written sentences as a game. Simply make an "I love" card with the letters about 1 in (2.5 cm) high. Line up three or four noun cards, as shown right, and get him to play the sentence game. Move the "I love" card in front of each noun as you say each sentence. Let him repeat it. Then ask him to show you the words that mean "I love Mommy," or "I like ice-cream."

How it helps your child to learn

This is a really simple way to introduce sentences.

I love	Daddy
I like	dinosaurs
I eat	ice-cream
Hello,	Johnny

Note: Sentence game cards are at the back of this book.

Special tip

You can also place the nouns face-down in one pile, with the phrases separate. Draw one from each and let your child read the resulting sentence.

And another thing!

Think up as many introductory words as you can, "I listen to," "I drink," "I see," "I ride." Even nonsense sentences are fun.

Indoor treasure hunts

What to do

Write out four or five cards with clues and place the first one somewhere, semi-hidden, perhaps jutting out from under a carpet.

The first clue leads to where the next clue card is placed. "Look where Mommy keeps the eggs," or "Clue number two is where you sleep." Then, "The treasure is near where Bobby sits when he is watching television."

The final clue says where the treasure is.

How it helps your child to learn

Treasure hunts teach reading and should build suspense—just like a book.

Special tip

For four-year-olds, make the clues fairly easy to find and follow. Make the clues tougher for older children

And another thing!

Older children appreciate rhyming clues—"Something red near the bed," "The next good news is linked with shoes."

"Race tracks" for reading

What to do

A "race track" game such as *Snakes and Ladders* can be used to really motivate reading.

For instance, take a pack of postcards and write an instruction on each: "Hop like a frog," "Flap your arms like a bird," "Twirl like a dancer."

You and your child turn over each one in turn, read it, act it out, and then move your counter along the board, one, two, or three squares, depending on how well he has mimed the instruction—the family makes the vote.

Special tip

Of course, *Snakes and Ladders* is a great aid for counting and adding. If the game really captures the family's imagination, get your child to either write down or suggest his own instructions.

How it helps your child to learn

Combines counting, action, and reading.

Some sample instructions

Keep the early instruction cards simple, then gradually more challenging—but always keep them fun. Some examples:

Cry like a baby.

Roar like a lion.

Walk around the room with a book on your head.

Pretend you're a fish in a river.

Imagine you are a rooster strutting around the yard.

Pretend you are a racing car driver screeching round a bend.

Word jigsaw puzzles

What to do

Write words that contain two, three or four syllables on individual cards. Make sure to write them with a gap between each syllable. Then cut between each syllable in a jigsaw pattern, making sure that they are split the same as in speech. Now get your child to assemble them.

How it helps your child to learn

Your child will have learned already to recognize many words by sight and to decode many others by simple phonetics. This game will enable him to grasp the phonic principle through physical handling.

Special tip

Start with one word at a time, then the components of two words together, so it becomes slightly more challenging.

And another thing!

Suggest he sounds out each syllable as he puts the word together, so he is learning by touch, speech, and sound at the same time.

The full sentence game

What to do

Play the sentence game with your child. Using the cards at the back of the book, the idea is to build full sentences. You'll find some sentence starters, middles, and endings. Each sentence is in the present tense. You can convert it to the past tense e.g., "Mommy and I **went** shopping yesterday."

How it helps your child to learn

Not only is this a stimulating composition game and spelling aid, but it can provide hundreds—in fact thousands—of different combination sentences.

My friends	are coming	to my party.
Airplanes	fly high	in the sky.
The bird	takes a bath	in the pool.
Our cat	likes to drink	warm milk.
The teacher	helps us to	read a book.
My mother	likes to	go shopping.

The who and what parts of each sentence are complete, so you can start with these. The starting phrases begin with a capital letter. The finishing phrases end in a period.

Special tip

Don't be worried if some of the sentence combinations end up as "nonsense." Children love that kind of play.

And another thing!

Keep each of the three sentence segments in a separate box, so you can play with as many pieces as you wish at any one time.

Sounds the same

What to do

Your child will already be using many combination letters in her speech: digraphs (two letters which join together to make a sound, as in **sh**, **th**, or **ch**) or phonograms (group letters which generally sound the same, such as **arch**, **all**, **ight**, **ank.**) Now introduce them as a simple rhyming game. Write one word on a blackboard, whiteboard, or a sheet of paper, and see how many matching words you can find.

How it helps your child to learn

It's a simple way to expand language through phonics.

Simple combinations

aw	**ck**	**ew**	**oo**	**wh**
saw	kick	crew	moo	what
jaw	neck	few	boot	when
law	back	flew	tooth	why
ay	**ee**	**ow**	**sh**	**ou**
say	tree	cow	shop	out
day	see	how	fish	ouch
pay	feed	down	shut	house
ch	**er**	**oa**	**th**	**ng**
chick	mother	boat	the	sing
chair	sister	soap	this	bring
itch	water	soak	then	finger

Special tip

Turn each example into a word game—"He lay on his back, with his neck on a sack, and kicked the clock."

And another thing!

Use books of children's poetry—and adults' as well—to show how words can rhyme, whether or not they are spelled the same.

Four reading games

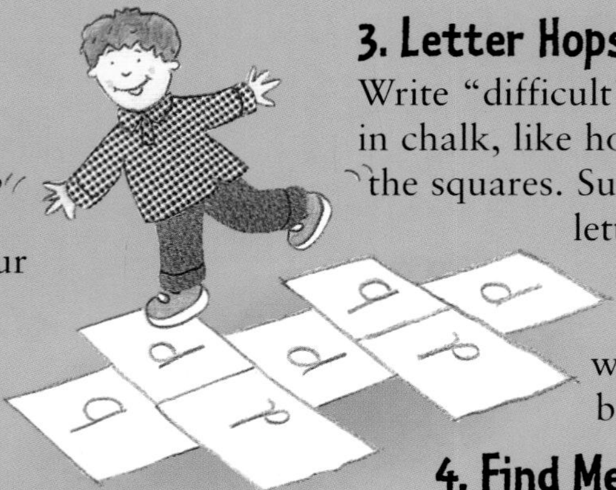

1. Simple word search

Write down a string of random letters, including a special word in it several times. Say, "I can see the word **dad** four times in these letters, can you?"

pbedadfgmsdadkjtvdadspdadwitx

2. Word Hunt

If your child can't tell the difference between **as** or **an**, **b** and **p**, play "Hunt the **an**" or "Hunt the **p**." Look at a big-type book and see how many times you can find the word.

3. Letter Hopscotch

Write "difficult" letters, such as **p**, **b**, and **d**, in chalk, like hopscotch, but with letters in the squares. Suggest your child hops to the letter that starts a word, such as "pull," and so on. Try writing sentences that start with the same letter e.g., "big blue balloon bubbles."

4. Find Me

For example, "Find me the word that (starts with **pl**)... Find me the word that is the opposite of (empty)" and so on.

Special tip

Look for opportunities to play with words in a fun way. Do crossword puzzles together—simple ones at first. Then try making up your own.

And another thing

Play I spy! e.g., "I spy a word beginning with **b** and ending with **ing**."

Four-minute reading program

What to do

If your child can recognize **b**'s, but is having problems distinguishing **d**'s from **p**'s, try writing a list of say 10 words that begin with **p** and/or include **p**'s: *paper, pepper, pet, puppy, parsnip, prune, prince, puppet.*

On the next night, create a list of words beginning with **d**. Spend only four minutes each night on each list. Each morning go through the list again together.

How it helps your child to learn

A nightly word list is a proven way to solve reading problems.

Special tip

If your child can pronounce the problem letters, but has difficulty in recognizing them, get him to dictate a funny sentence to you, using examples of the letters.

And another thing!

Children who have English as a second language often recognize words that begin or end with certain letters and sounds.

Writing

"Teaching your children to read, write, and spell is fun."

Peter Young and Colin Tyre in **Teach Your Child To Read.**

Writing

Learning to write is almost as easy as learning to read. In fact, some children find it easier. The reason is twofold:

1. Children can **explode** into writing, virtually without any instruction, if they have the equipment and activities to develop pre-writing ability.
2. They find writing easier because they are expressing their own thoughts, while in reading they have to understand the thoughts of others.

The three aspects to writing

How you write —The physical ability to use a crayon, pencil, or pen to print words, or later to write them in flowing, linked script—and later again to type them on a word processor.

What you write—The ability to put your thoughts on paper.

Getting it right —The ability to spell, punctuate, and link sentences so they make sense.

All three skills can be developed naturally. Most children can master the physical skills of printing before starting school. The FUNdamentals program makes this easy.

Writing starts with the coordination skills a child can learn from very early play.

The materials we recommend are designed to prepare each child **indirectly** for future writing. For example, knobs on puzzles encourage the child to lift and manipulate them, coordinating his finger and thumb.

Making letters

Buy some of the excellent plastic letters which are available, often with raised, stippled surfaces or with magnetic strips for leaving messages on refrigerator doors.

Or you can make the letters yourself by cutting them out of sandpaper.

By tracing sandpaper letters with his fingers, he will develop a “muscle memory” of the patterns for forming letters.

Make each letter about 3 in. (7.5 cm) high, and glue it on to cardboard squares approximately 6 in. x 6 in. (15 cm x 15 cm.) Make two of each lower-case letter, one of each capital letter and one of each numeral from 0 to 9.

You can introduce your child to stippled or sandpaper letters at any time between three and four years, or even earlier if you'd like to associate the feel of letters with learning the alphabet.

So, when you're telling your child the letters that spell "ball," guide his hand over the letters, in the same direction he will later write them.

Make the sandpaper letters in the same style as we have printed the early Noun or Verb Cards. It's called the cursive style. You'll notice that the letters have little "tails" as in **t** or **a**. This makes it easier for your child to make the transition to "joined up" writing when he gets to school.

Play letter games

Have fun playing pre-writing games: tracing letters in the air with big hand movements, or tracing them by holding your child's finger and directing him to show which way the letters go—even before he starts to write.

Between three and four years, it's time for a movable alphabet: a box with all the letters of the alphabet, preferably with the consonants in one color and the vowels in another.

You should ask your child to tell you which words he would like to spell. Or you can suggest words that cover all the sounds of the English language.

These sounds are **all** contained in these words: *cat, dog, fish, pig, sun, bed, rabbit, leg, three, man, snake, bar, jump, hand, wagon, yard, moon, kite, zipper, straw, smoke, turtle, chair, house, oil, horse, wheel, uniform, book, and butter.*

As well as making words like this with your movable alphabet, you can write each word on a separate page of a scrapbook, and play a game to find and write down words that rhyme with those on the list.

The "explosion" begins

If you start the pre-writing exercises while the child is also being exposed to nouns, verbs, and labels, he will almost certainly "explode" into writing at his own pace. His writing will develop as naturally as his spoken language did at an earlier stage.

When the explosion into writing begins, make sure to have plenty of sheets, or a large roll of white paper on hand, and lots of colored pencils and crayons. Once your child masters the physical act of writing, your priority will be to encourage him to *want* to write. There are ideas for this on the cards that follow.

Within a short while of your child learning to write, she will be finding every available opportunity to scribble, draw, or write using her newly discovered skills!

Using the writing templates

What to do

When your child can hold a crayon well enough to scribble and is dabbing paint on paper with a brush, start him with the templates like the one shown here.

Get him to draw inside the shapes with a thick pencil or felt pen, so it makes an outline. Then fill in the shape first with solid colors, then by drawing vertical, horizontal or diagonal lines inside the shape he's produced (Fig 2.)

Be lavish, but constructive, in your praise e.g., "Well done, it looks good because you held your pencil properly this time."

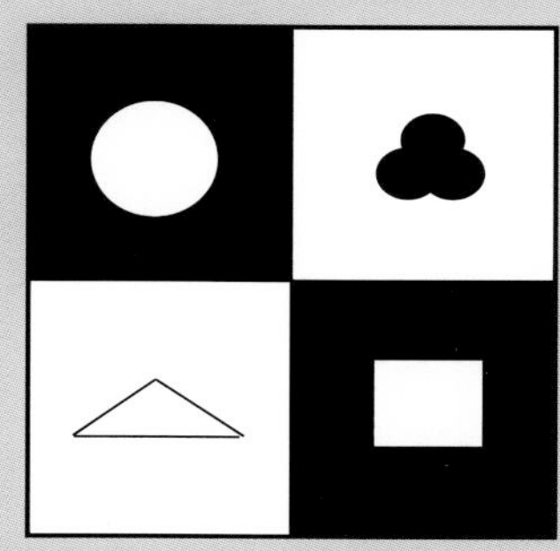

Fig 1

How it helps your child to learn

When your child can master these shapes at a smaller size, he's just about ready to "explode" into writing.

Fig 2

Special tip

Once he can trace inside the templates, take the pieces that have been cut out and get him to run his pencil around the **outside**.

And another thing!

Note that all the shapes for printed letters are contained in the templates for a square, a triangle, a circle, and a clover leaf.

Making shapes

What to do

Help her to draw shapes in freehand and make pictures composed of squares, oblongs, circles, triangles, ovals, and curves. Look for shapes in picture books, in the house, and outdoors.

How it helps your child to learn

The English alphabet uses only straight lines, circles, and curves. Once she can draw these, she is close to letter formation.

Special tip

Suggest she makes, for example, all the circles red, all the squares green. She's sorting as well as preparing for writing.

And another thing!

Suggest she draws a train, a house, a car, or a person, using only recognizable shapes like oblongs, circles, and triangles.

Follow the dots

What to do

When he can make shapes well and has used the templates, he's ready for formal writing. Start by making the letters out of dots following the directions that the letters should be formed in. Explain where to start and how to follow the dots the way the arrows point.

How it helps your child to learn

This activity helps him understand the shape and direction of the letters.

Special tip

It's worth asking an art shop to laminate a set for you. Then he can go over them again and again by wiping them clean with a felt-tip pen.

And another thing!

When he can form the letters, give him lots of words where he can complete the word by filling in the initial letter (as above.)

Writing his own name

What to do

At three or four, most children learn to write their own names, even if in rudimentary form. Use this three-step process:

1. Using a thick felt marker or crayon, write the child's name on a large sheet of cardboard. The child writes over the letters with crayon, with your hand guiding his.
2. Write the name again and cover it with tracing paper. Let him trace over it.
3. Write his name lightly in pencil, letting him write over it.

How it helps your child to learn

Nothing seems to inspire writing more than starting with the word that means most to a child.

Special tip

As a general rule, print letters about 2 in. (5 cm) deep for a start, and then gradually make them smaller as competence improves.

And another thing!

Progress to writing special words—a pet's name, a friend's name, a shopping list, or a present list.

Triple letters

What to do

When your child starts to reduce the size of her printing, you can help her with this simple triple-writing exercise. Get her to choose three different pencils from her colored pencil collection.

Suggest getting her to write something silly or funny, such as "green gorillas" or "smiling snakes." Either you or she can write out the first letter with one pencil, and then she can copy it with a different color, and then another.

How it helps your child to learn

A few fantasy words and some extra color make learning much easier and more motivating.

g
g
green
gorillas

Special tip

If your child has brought some letters home from nursery school to write, use those to make up your fantasy words.

And another thing!

If you're short of words, try *raging rhino, purple piano, bashful budgie, concrete lollipop, or sandy ice-cream.*

Back writing

What to do

If your child sometimes confuses one letter with another in writing (say **b** and **d**), take a large sheet of paper and stick it on a smooth wall. Give him a thick felt-tip pen and put him in a position where he can hold out his arm and write on the sheet.

Stand behind him and use your index finger to write that letter, very large, on his back. Tell him, "That's a b." Get him to repeat it, and write it on the paper. Teach only one letter at a time until it's correct.

How it helps your child to learn

This method creates "muscle memory" for letters. (You can also "write" on the back of his hand.)

Try writing a letter on his back—he must guess it.

Special tip

Do each letter a second time, naming the strokes. "**B** says buh. First, draw a stick. Then, add a ball." Repeat if needed.

And another thing!

Some children may have poor hand-eye coordination, and this method helps them as much as those who may confuse letters.

Beginnings and endings

What to do

Create cards about 1 in (2.5 cm) square and write various consonants on them e.g.:

b **d** **f** **h** **m** **p**

Then make up some word endings, such as these.

ood **ear** **ow**

The game is to see how often you can combine a single "beginning" letter to the "ending" letters.

Examples

Which of these starters

b **s** **t** **w**

can combine with these endings?

ear **ill**
in **end**

Special tip

Other board games, such as *Boggle* and *Junior Scrabble,* are great for slightly older children.

And another thing!

Extend the game by using "blended" beginnings: **pl, tr, gr, cl, sl,** and **ch** with endings like **ead, ink, ash, ade,** and **amp**.

Motivation to write

What to do

Once she can write, look for reasons why she would want to write (and read.) Here are some:

1. A mail box at home to exchange notes
2. Copy down a recipe, or a verse from a nursery rhyme or song
4. A Christmas or birthday present list
5. Write a short story
6. A letter to grandma
7. Rhyming phrases, like "Bill sees a pill on a hill"
8. A list of things to do, or a shopping list
9. A sign for her door (e.g., KEEP OUT!)

When she writes a story, give lots of specific praise and ask simple questions that encourage her to develop her story further.

Special tip

Let her dictate a short story to you—her name, where she lives, her pets, etc. Then write it down in big, clear letters in light pencil.

And another thing!

Let her read back her own mini-story and then trace over the letters you formed in pencil. It's now her own story!

Math

"All the arithmetical expressions we know of consist of only 10 symbols."

Don Fabun in **Three Roads to Awareness.**

Making math fun

Counting is the starting point of almost all mathematics. So get into the habit of counting everything with your pre-schooler. The buttons on her coat, potatoes on the plate, steps, jumps, red cars passing on a journey, birds on a tree.

Clapping is an ideal way for her to record the concept of numbers in a physical sense. Clap and count at the same time.

Cooking is also an ideal time to talk naturally about numbers. "Let's cut this pizza into four quarters. Let's cut it in half first. Then cut it in half again. That's four pieces." Or, "We need three potatoes. Let's cut each one in half. That makes six halves. One, two …"

Weigh her regularly and mark down her weight on a chart. Measure her height in the same way and talk out loud about how much extra she has grown. Ask her to weigh her toys. Which one is the heaviest? How many toys weigh a pound? Give her directions to find something in the garden. "Take four big jumps forward, now turn to the left and take six big strides. Now turn and do nine hops forward."

This type of game is especially valuable as she is learning through her senses and this "muscle memory" is very strong.

Mathematics is about concepts, too—like longer, shorter, more, less, heavier and lighter, nearer, and farther.

Let your child experience the concepts—"This is the cold water. Let's put some hot water in and make it a bit warmer. Now a bit more—see it's hotter still."

Math is also about sorting and classifying. So let him help to match up socks by color, separate shirts from blouses and sort the knives, spoons, and forks. And make shell or stone collections that he can sort by size, shape, or color. Seeing patterns is a very important math concept.

Also get used to talking about shapes all the time. You can make shapes with a glue pen and sprinkle sand over the glue.

He will come to recognize the shapes quickly because you are teaching in a multi-sensory way. You can do the same thing for the numerals—and trace them on his back.

Only when he understands that two means two of something should you introduce him to written numbers.

Do so with special number cards. Make them so that they have dots on one side and the equivalent numeral on the reverse, so he can count or add the dots first and then check out the number on the back.

Once he knows his numbers, playing shop or simple board games like *Snakes and Ladders* is great practice.

Learn shapes by feel

What to do

You can start teaching children the names of shapes—by how they feel.

Simply assemble a number of objects that are square (a cracker, the lid of a box), round (a biscuit, the lid of a jar), and a triangle (a cut sandwich, a folded table napkin.) Ask your child to feel each one as you tell him what it is. Then use the three-step learning process to reinforce the message.

How it helps your child to learn

Learning is quicker when you involve more than one sense, and also involve "muscle memory."

Special tip

Keep it simple at first, "This is a triangle. This is a square." Then gradually expand, "A triangle always has three sides."

And another thing!

Move gradually onto other shapes: rectangles, octagons, and all the different types of triangle.

The biggest/ smallest game

What to do

Play a game of finding the biggest and smallest items around your home or garden. For example, suggest children find the biggest and smallest book in the house, the biggest and smallest painting or picture, the biggest and smallest pot, chair, house plant, and window. For outside, the biggest and smallest tree, stone, plant, and flower.

How it helps your child to learn

This activity encourages powers of observation, and it helps children categorize by size—another basic principle of mathematics.

Special tip

This is also a good game to play at children's parties. Print the lists in advance. The first to complete the list wins a prize.

And another thing!

After biggest and smallest, you can introduce the principles of "big, bigger, biggest" and "small, smaller, smallest."

Shape hunts

What to do

Suggest a "shape hunt" when you're out. How many triangles can you find? How many circles? (such as road signs, wheels, steering wheels.)

Then have an indoor "shape hunt." Draw the basic shapes on a sheet of white paper, as shown on the right. Your child marks a stroke for each shape she can find.

How it helps your child to learn

This is an excellent introduction to recognizing and counting categories. Ruling a line through each group of four strokes to count five is a good introduction to Roman numerals.

Special tip

Move on later to more complex shapes, such as pentagons, hexagons, and octagons. Check them in an encyclopedia.

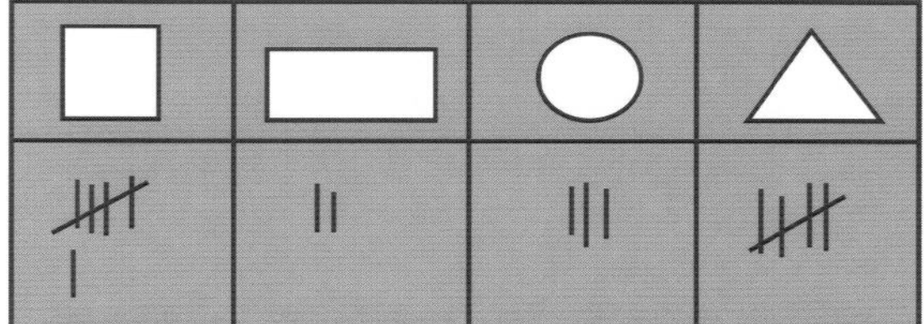

Introducing number dominoes

What to do

Dominoes are excellent for counting. You can make a set slightly larger than a bought set, as shown on the right, with white cards 4 in x 2 in (10 cm x 5 cm.) Draw a line through the middle and use plain dots from 0 to 6 in (0 to 15 cm) each square (1 + 2, 2 + 3, 2 + 2, 3 + 3 and so on.)

Turn the cards face-down in equal piles. Then take turns to turn a domino up from your own pile, and see if it can be matched to either of the end dominoes. If not, you must keep your domino until you can.

The first to use all his dominoes wins. You can also hunt for dominoes where the dots add to a previously-agreed number.

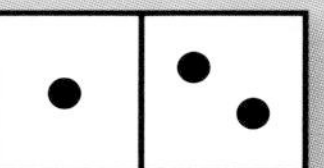

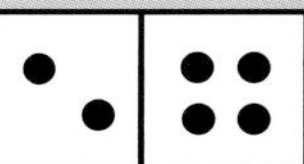

How it helps your child to learn

This is excellent for associating dots with specific numbers.

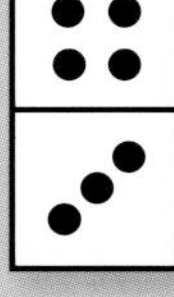

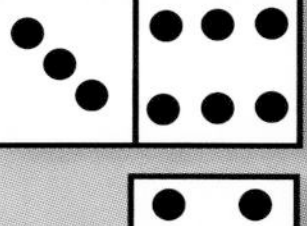

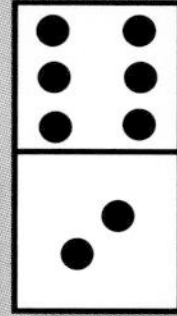

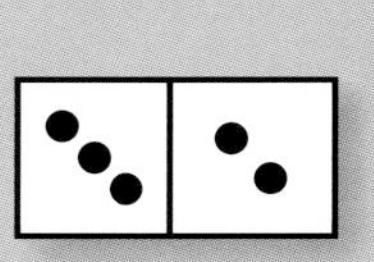

Special tip

Make sure to say the numbers as each one is turned up, so that your child can recognize the names for the numbers. "That's a three and a four."

And another thing!

For many children, money makes math seem logical. So give your child pocket money and help him manage it.

Weigh everything

What to do

Ask your child which weighs more, a pound of butter or a pound of sugar? Get out the scales. What's the heaviest? An orange or potato? Which is the lightest apple? How much more does a potato weigh than a grape? What's the heaviest vegetable in the house? Which is the largest soft toy? How much does Teddy weigh?

Weigh and measure lots of things. Make a bar chart to compare them.

How it helps your child to learn

This is good for introducing the concepts of both weight and volume.

Special tip

Children under four nearly always think bigger-bulk items weigh more. From four onward, they're open to proof.

And another thing!

Under-fours think a tall thinner glass holds more water than a short fatter one of the same volume.

Real and "play" shopping

What to do

Between age three and four, children love to play shop. You can now buy plastic cash registers, play money, sets of plastic and cardboard price tickets and even imitation cartons and packets. These make excellent third birthday presents. Of course you can easily use empty boxes and your own price tickets.

On real shopping trips, discuss prices and why you decide on what you buy, why some out-of-season fruit is expensive and what makes a bargain.

How it helps your child to learn

Shopping is an excellent introduction to the role of money and mathematics—and budgeting children's allowance.

Special tip

Let your child pay for ice cream or drinks so she understands what money is for and learns about change.

And another thing!

Take 5 pennies and show her they are the same as a nickel. Do the same for 10 and 25 cents.

Learning fractions

What to do

A good starting point is folding paper napkins, in half, then in quarters. Then cut pictures up into halves and quarters.

Next cut up a pizza or a pie. The pizza is a real multi-sensory experience—especially if you make it yourself and talk through the herbs and smells and ingredients.

Fruit, like melon, pumpkin, or pineapple, slices up well into halves, quarters and eighths.

How it helps your child to learn

This hands-on mathematics soon teaches that if you cut four quarters each in half, you get eighths, because 2 x 4 = 8.

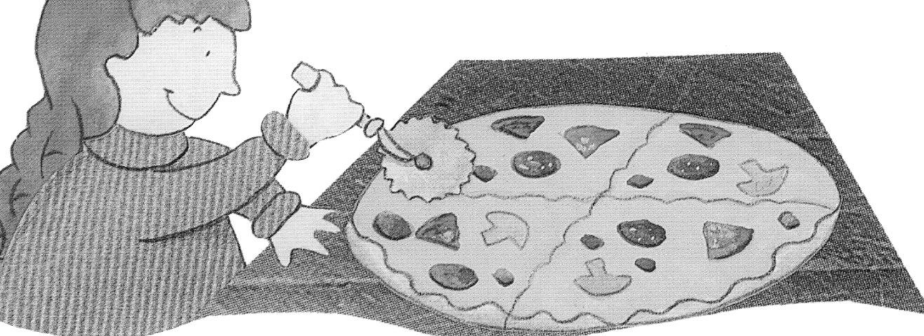

Special tip

Slice potatoes, carrots, and bread into fractions. Fold and cut paper, then paint the fractions. Almost any food can be cut into fractions.

And another thing!

Chocolate slabs provide a ready-made way of demonstrating fractions—and you can eat the right answer!

Play Bingo

What to do

To make sure children practice numbers from 1 to 100, you can play Bingo. Each player has a card with a small selection of numbers, plus some counters. The caller has a bag of marbles or cards, numbered from 1 to 100, and pulls those numbers out one at a time. Each player puts a counter over any number on his card that has been called. The first player with a full card wins.

How it helps your child to learn

Even small children can learn their numbers from 1 to 100 through Bingo. It's good for concentration, too.

Make your own Bingo

Make your own family Bingo game by:

1. Dividing up a board, about 12 in (30 cm) square, into 100 squares: 10 columns of 10, numbered 1 to 100.
2. Cutting up a similarly-numbered board into 100 numbered counters.
3. Make 10 cards, about 5 in x 4 in (12.5 cm x 10 cm) each, with 20 numbers chosen at random between 1 and 20. Make four rows of five numbers in total.
4. Provide 20 markers or counters for each player.

Special tip

When you're starting to play Bingo with a smaller child, it often helps if an adult partners him for the first few games.

And another thing!

You can vary the rules by announcing that the winner of the next game needs to have only a completed row across or down.

Adding with Math Grid One

What to do

Put the board on the table with a pile of coins or counters. Put two counters on one side, one on the other. Ask, "How many on this side? How many on that side? How many altogether? That's right, 2 and 1 makes 3."

Then add them together on one side of the grid. As he progresses, he will see that 5 + 4 is the same as 6 + 3, 7 + 2, etc. You can throw counters on the board to make it more of a game.

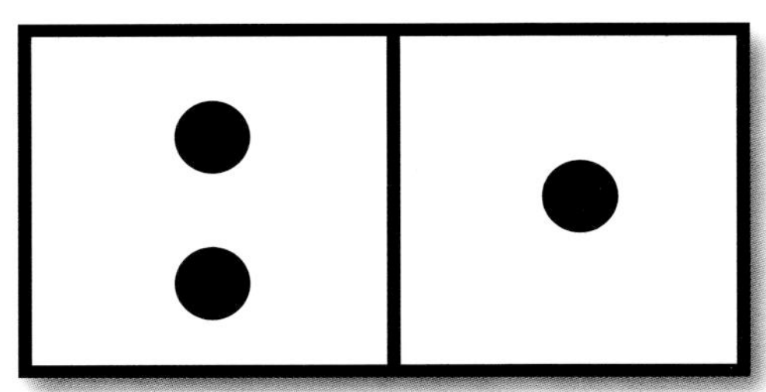

Math Grid One in use

How it helps your child to learn

Make math physical and real. Make it a game and he'll grow up to enjoy it.

Special tip

Ensure he understands that 1 + 2 = 3 and so does 2 + 1. Always ensure he physically counts each counter by placing his finger on each one.

And another thing!

When he knows all the adding combinations up to 10 (they are called number bonds,) turn the game into taking away. Put, for example, 5 counters on one side. Move one counter off the board saying, "5 take away 1 is...?"

Adding and Dividing with Math Grid Two

What to do

Start with six counters and let her count them. Then place them on the board in different squares (as Fig 1.) Ask how many in each square. Answer: 3, 2 and 1.

Say, "Right—so 3 plus 2 plus 1 is 6. How many other ways can we make 6? (or 8? or 10?)"

Fig 1

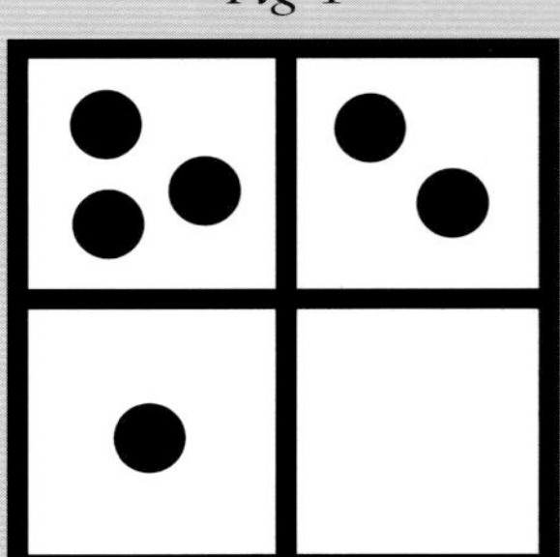

Fig 2

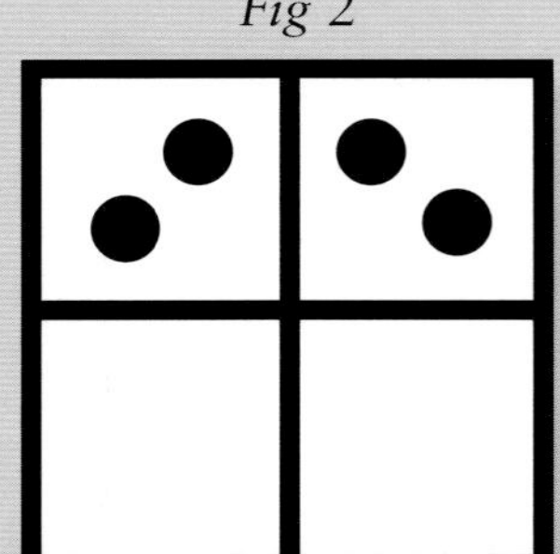

Math Grid Two in use

How it helps your child to learn

Gets her used to the idea that any number is made up of lots of other numbers.

Special tip

Stay with adding—and subtracting—for a long time. You can introduce the idea of dividing very simply along the way.

And another thing!

Take four counters. Put two counters in each of two squares (as in Fig 2.) Say, "Look, we started with 4 counters, then we shared or divided them between these two squares. We say 4 divided by 2 is 2." Repeat it lots of times with other combinations of numbers e.g., 6, 8, 9, 10.

Playing card battles

What to do

Take a pack of cards with the face or picture cards removed. Divide into two halves and place the two piles face-down in front of each player. The players turn over the top card of their packs simultaneously. The players must add up the total of the two cards. The first to shout out wins. Start with 1's, 2's and 3's. Keep the additions below ten until she's really confident.

How it helps your child to learn

This game encourages your child to develop fast recognition of number values.

Special Tip

Alternatives: Take the cards from 1-10. She must put them in sequence. Or, pull out a card—what comes before it, what after it?

And another thing!

To make it even harder (age 5+) the players deduct the lower number from the highest. The first with the answer wins.

Math food games

What to do

Food is also a great tool for introducing math concepts. Here are three ideas:

The more or less game

a. I've got 4 sweets, you've got 2. Have you got more or less?

b. We started with 10 sweets. We've eaten 3. Have we got more or less than we started with?

c. I've got 4 potatoes on the plate, you've got 3. If we put them together, will there be more or less than 4?

Special tip

For younger children, start with books that have detailed pictures so you can encourage the child to find visual answers.

And another thing!

If a young child has difficulty answering questions, lead into some possible answers yourself: "I wonder if he's..."

Mad Menus

What to do

Make up a menu on your whiteboard—or on paper. Make the menu crazy and fun. Draw the items if she can't read everything.

Give her some pennies and ask what she wants to order. How much does it cost? Has she enough to buy what she wants?

How it helps your child to learn

This kind of activity is good fun and presents a "real" use of math.

Special tip

Graduate to other coins (pennies, nickels, dimes, and quarters) as she gets more proficient so that she will also get an understanding of how money works.

And another thing!

Make up a story about wacky characters coming into the restaurant and ordering disgusting food.

Exploring patterns

What to do

Use counters to make patterns. Start by placing some counters, as in Fig 1, and ask, "What's the pattern here? What will the next line look like?" Play the game using columns of counters that progress: 2, 4, 6, 8, etc. Always ask, "What will the next line look like?"

Then try patterns that involve subtraction (see Fig 2) and progression in twos or threes (see Fig 3.)

How it helps your child to learn

She'll realize that there are patterns to numbers, and that they can be fun and interesting.

Special tip

Use your whiteboard or blackboard to show a pattern in actual numbers: 2, 4, 6, 8. Ask what comes next.

Fig 1

Fig 2

Fig 3

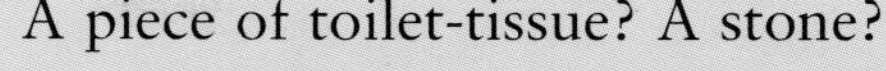

Stopwatch fun

What to do

Use a stopwatch to find out:

- How many hops/somersaults can you do in a minute? Guess first. How near were you? How many in two minutes?
- How long does it take to climb a ladder? Fill a bucket of water? Write your name? Walk round the room? Sing the alphabet song? Guess first. How near were you?
- How long does it take for a feather to float to the ground? A leaf? A piece of toilet-tissue? A stone?
- How many things can you do in three minutes? Sing Humpty Dumpty twice? Count up to 100? Write A to K?

How it helps your child to learn

Counting and concepts of time become fun and relevant.

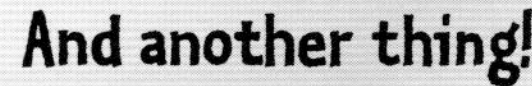

Special tip

Encourage her to keep making forecasts and to get more and more accurate with practice.

And another thing!

Use an egg timer to let her practice guessing the elapse of time. Then show what the same time period is on a clock.

Tens and Ones

What to do

Make up a rod divided into units as illustrated.

1. Count the units on the 10 rod.
2. Make up another 10 rod and place it beside the first and invite her to say or count what the total is.
3. Write 20 on a piece of paper, place it by the rods and say that 20 is two tens.
4. Then bring in a single unit square to place beside the two tens and invite her to say or count the new total. Write 21 on a piece of paper. Continue until she really understands the idea.

How it helps your child to learn

This activity prepares your child for working in units and tens.

Special tip

On another day, use counters, popcorn, or raisins to group in 10's.

And another thing!

Regularly count from 10 to 100 in tens as she puts on her pajamas—and back again.

Number games

What to do

Make number games a natural part of every day by playing games like these:

Forward and Backward

This is played like a tennis match. One player starts counting—the next adds or subtracts one from the previous total (see example A.) You can vary this by adding or subtracting 2's or 3's, as in example B.

How it helps your child to learn

Good math students must become absolutely fluent in adding or subtracting any number.

A **1,** 2, **3,** 4, **5,** 6, **7,** 8, **7,** 8, **9,** 8, **9,** 10, **9,** 10, **11** . . .

B **1,** 4, **7,** 10, **7,** 10, **13,** 16 . . .

Special tip

Adding or subtracting 10 is a good start to decimals.

And another thing!

You should initially put the numbers from 0 to 20 on a piece of paper to help.

Animal adding

What to do

The idea is to turn addition into something fun and concrete. Have your child add the legs of animals—for example, add the legs of a bird to the legs of an octopus.

Answer: 10

How it helps your child to learn

Children love doing anything connected with animals. This activity shows that counting is not an abstract activity but is relevant in the "real world."

Other examples:

What's the total number of legs of:

A horse and a bird? Answer: 4 + 2 = 6

A dog and a cat? Answer: 4 + 4 = 8

A bird and a spider? Answer: 2 + 8 = 10

A bee and a cat? Answer: 6 + 4 = 10

Three birds and a cow? Answer: 2 + 2 + 2 + 4 = 10

Special tip

Encourage drawing stick figures to work out the problem. It prompts visual thinking.

And another thing!

You could even make songs out of the sums.

Measure—everything!

What to do

Erect a big wall poster (of thick cardboard) to contain all your child's measurements, and not just the obvious ones—height, length of legs, arms, fingers, and feet, hand-span, circumference of waist, chest, thighs, collar, and around the head.

Then use these measurements to compare with others around the house—width of doors, cabinets, height of chairs, and tables.

Alternative: Use a pencil as a unit of measure, too—"How many pencil lengths is the door, your arm, the cat?"

How it helps your child to learn

As with most things, measurement principles are learnt most easily when they relate to oneself.

Special tip

Decorate your measurement poster with traced outlines of your child's hands and feet.

And another thing!

Use tape measures and rulers to demonstrate measurement.

Counting in the street

What to do

When your child is starting to recognize double-digit numbers, point them out as you are walking outside. Walk out on the "even numbers" side of the street, and back on the "odds."

If your house is number 4, then mention that the next will be number 6, and then 8. Get him used to the idea of predicting what number comes next, and you can make the lesson simple by pointing out the intervening number on the other side.

How it helps your child to learn

An excellent introduction to odd and even numbers.

Special tip

Get him to add the numbers, too, so that number 20 becomes 2+0=2. And 22 becomes 2+2= 4, etc.

Special tip

Counting the numbers backward will of course help teach subtraction.

Using dot and numeral cards

What to do

Make cards with numbers, patterns of dots, and math symbols or use the ones at the back of this book. They are an introduction to the sort of math that she will do in school. For example, you can put a four-dot card and a three-dot card together as illustrated and say that 4 + 3 = 7. Get her to repeat it and **count the dots to check.**

Keep the + sign and the = sign in place, and make a game out of replacing the first two cards with new dot cards and asking her to find the card with the answer.

When she has done the sum correctly, turn over the cards so they now display numerals. When you think she is ready, play only with the number cards. She can always check her answers by checking against the cards with the dots and counting them.

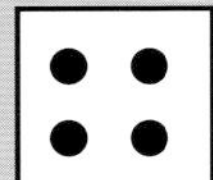 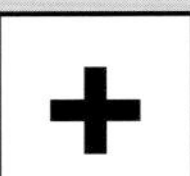 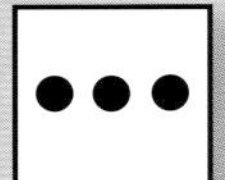 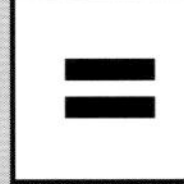 

4  3 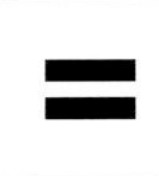 7

Special tip

When she is happy with this type of adding sum, you can show her that the sum is the same whether you lay out the sum from left to right, or vertically.

And another thing!

Create separate piles of number cards, addition or subtraction signs and equals signs. Make your own sums.

Counting contests

What to do

Challenge your child to a dinosaur competition: "I bet I can say more 'tyrannosauruses' while you count from 20 to 0 than you can say 'tyrannosauruses' while I count from 20 to 0."

If he accepts, take a strip of paper and write the numerals 0 to 20 from left to right. He'll have to find 20 and work backward. While he counts down, you say "tyrannosauruses" over and over, and on a separate piece of paper, make a mark each time you say it. Then it's his turn.

How it helps your child to learn

Practices the basic ability to count.

Special tip

Get your child to create his own things to count. Count forward as well as backward.

And another thing!

There are obvious variations on this theme e.g.,

1. How many numbers can you write, starting at one and counting forward, while I count backward from 32 to 11?
2. How far can you walk backward while I count from 50 to 100?
3. How many coins can you toss into a hat while I count from 38 to 18? Now reverse the roles.

Creativity

"No family is too poor to switch off the television and talk together."

The Rev. Jesse Jackson.

Creativity

One of the major factors for success in the 21st century will be creativity. Huge amounts of information are already a few key strokes away on the Internet. It's the people who are able to analyze that information logically and see fresh implications in it, who will have a head start.

So to encourage and extend the natural inventiveness of your child is to give her a gift that will last a lifetime.

The first seven years will determine much of your child's willingness to create, invent, question, and above all to see common situations in many different ways.

Creativity spans the whole field of human endeavor. It's not just in music, art, or writing, it's in cooking, laying out a garden, inventing new products, and ways of doing things. Seeing what everyone else has seen, but seeing it in a new way. All it takes is to give your child an environment that encourages imagination. For example:

- Regularly explore the countryside.
- Build models together from old boxes, yogurt pots, toilet roll tubes, and bits of wood.
- Play games that involve the senses—identifying perfumes, colors, textures, tastes.
- Have daily art sessions that go beyond coloring books, and include things like finger painting.
- Encourage dressing-up games, stage shows, and role-play games—make-believe restaurants where she feeds pets or toys; schools where she teaches her teddies to count; stores where she can count money and practice her writing on receipts, and jobs like train driver, vet, submarine captain, nurse, fireman, detective, or farmer.

- Use lots of sensory words—so a color isn't just green, but lime green or pine-needle green.

Your use of words like these will bring out her creative use of language when she comes to write stories.

A child whose parents are always wondering why and how, and, "if we did that I wonder what would happen?" has a great role-model for creativity.

Art supply box

You don't need to spend a fortune on art supplies to encourage artistic creativity. Your child will probably be happier creating binoculars, space rockets, or puppets out of toilet-tissue tubes than he will be with expensive toys. Here are some items that can be saved or used in a creative "art supplies" box:

- Aluminum foil
- Aluminum trays
- Beads
- Beans
- Bottle caps
- Boxes
- Buttons
- Candles
- Chalk
- Clothes' pegs
- Coins
- Cotton wool
- Crêpe paper
- Dowelling
- Driftwood
- Egg cartons
- Feathers
- Felt
- Film containers
- Floor tiles
- Food coloring
- Glitter
- Greeting cards
- Gummed stars
- Jar lids
- Leather scraps
- Lentils
- Lollipop sticks
- Magazines
- Matchsticks (used)
- Milk cartons
- Paper cups
- Pasta shapes
- Pebbles
- Pipe cleaners
- Plastic boxes
- Plastic jars
- Plastic tubs
- Plasticine
- Plates and tubes
- Popcorn
- Ribbon
- Sand
- Sandpaper
- Shells
- Shoelaces
- Soap (for sculptures)
- Sponge
- Stamp pad
- Stamps
- Straws
- Streamers
- String
- Styrofoam trays
- Tape
- Thread
- Toothpicks
- Velvet scraps
- Wallpaper scraps and samples
- Wine corks
- Wooden ice-cream spoons
- Woodscraps
- Yarn

Pictures from fabric

What to do

Always keep scraps from any sewing. And from time to time invite your youngster to make them into pictures by cutting them up and pasting them onto large sheets of cardboard.

Ask first, "What shall we make from these lovely colors?" If there's any hesitation, suggest, "How about a clown's face, or a rabbit? Which would you like?" Then help her to cut out the pieces, starting with the big bits first.

How it helps your child to learn

Develops the key, but often neglected, sense of feeling and touch, and encourages creativity.

Special tip

Use scissors with rounded points, and a paste-pot with a brush that fits through the screw-top, and something to catch the drips.

And another thing!

Encourage her to use bits of yarn, ribbon, wool, and velvet strips, although you may have to paste on the small ones for her.

New food ideas

What to do

Encourage your junior cook to be creative in food preparation. Start with open sandwiches. See how your child can create faces, with grapes or stuffed olives for eyes, serrated carrots or tomatoes for a mouth, and a stick of celery for hair.

See how other vegetables can be cut into different shapes. Carrot and potato slices can become car wheels. Spring onions can be sliced from the top and dipped in water so they sprout like palm trees. Work together to create pictures and models.

How it helps your child to learn

Encourages more creativity, using a new combination of old elements.

Special tip

Make a list of dishes your family eats regularly. Then have a brainstorming session to see how you can make them different.

And another thing!

Regularly involve him in all your cooking and he'll learn adding, subtracting, and all the units of dry and wet measurements.

Paint-Plus!

What to do

Brushes are just a starting point. Try:

Hands: Smear on paint and press on to paper to make patterns.

Vegetables: Press paint on cut potatoes, celery, or even fruit. Use as a stamp.

Roll-on deodorant bottle: Fill with paint and apply to wet and dry paper.

Eye-droppers: Fill with paint and squirt onto wet or dry paper.

Your child: Draw around your child on to the back of some spare wallpaper. He fills in the outline.

Glow paint: Mix one part powder paint with two parts detergent and two parts water.

Salt shakers: Shake out powder paint, salt, sand, or glitter for colorful effects. (You can also punch holes in a jar lid.)

Special tip

Mount a colored world map on to cardboard and cut it out like a jigsaw puzzle.

And another thing!

Paint stones to become faces. Paint fir cones and acorns. Make a twig sculpture and models out of clay and bake.

Plaster of Paris

What to do

Look in kitchenware, DIY and hobby shops for a variety of molds for cookies, candies, and garden ornaments. Then make your own plaster of Paris using two parts of plaster (from a paint or DIY shop) to one part of water.

Fill each mold with plaster of Paris, let it harden for about an hour and then remove. Your child can paint them with watercolor paints, either immediately or when they have dried for a few days.

How it helps your child to learn

Encourages creativity and artistic skills.

Special tip

Small molds can be turned into personal necklaces or ornaments. When the plaster is hard, drill through and add a ribbon.

And another thing!

Keep a lookout for special novelty molds, such as dinosaurs, animals, and cartoon characters.

Nature collages

What to do

Turn visits to the beach or a forest into creative adventures. Collect shells, driftwood, colored pebbles, seaweed, acorns, seeds, birds' feathers, flax, leaves, twigs, petals, and reeds. Back home, use poster board or the side of a big carton as a base.

What can she make from her collection—a rainbow, peacock's tail, swordfish, or tree pattern?

Encourage her to lay them out until she's satisfied. Then attach with non-toxic glue.

How it helps your child to learn

Observing and sorting are scientific activities.

Special tip

Particularly successful are abstract dried food collages—dried peas, beans, rice, herbs, pasta, and spices.

And another thing!

When the artwork is complete, make sure it's hung in a suitable place for all to admire—and don't forget the photographic record.

Magic of the mind

What to do

Ask your child if she'd like to play a new game, called Magic of the Mind. Mention that the mind can create almost anything, and suggest you both start by inventing a new animal, by combining features of other creatures like a cat with deer's antlers, a dog with wings, an elephant with zebra stripes, a crocodile with a deer's horns.

You can play Magic of the Mind in teams, in pairs, and with one child suggesting an answer and the other drawing it. What's the advantage of your new animal?

How it helps your child to learn

This sparks lots of creativity.

Special tip

If the children love this game, suggest it regularly, but with different subjects: new vehicles, fish, birds, buildings, or toys.

And another thing!

Progress from inventing new animals to describing space aliens!

A shape collage

What to do

Select some colorful paper from your recycling box—preferably bright wrapping paper. Cut it into squares, circles, triangles, stars, rectangles, and ovals. Provide a large sheet of cardboard, or a sheet of poster paper, plus some glue and invite your child to make up his own shape collage. Talk to him about what he might like to make—would he like to make them into a tree, a face, a house, a garden, a flower, a lion…?

How it helps your child to learn

He learns about relative sizes, and color combinations and develops the fine-motor skills valuable for pre-writing.

Special tip

As an alternative, cut out the same type of shapes and paste on paper plates. You can thread string through them to make masks.

And another thing!

Talk to your child later about how all life involves shapes: squares for windows and doors, circles for wheels, triangles for tents, etc.

Make your own maze

What to do

You can build your own maze with indoor and outdoor furniture. Line it up so children can crawl through it. Start with chairs, tables, boxes, or coiled plastic hoses. Add anything to make it more difficult or fun. Tie string or ropes so they crawl under without touching. Or place an empty pot or bucket so they have to wriggle past without disturbing it.

How it helps your child to learn

The physical act of crawling and creeping builds up the sense of balance and helps coordination, so it's a sensory activity, too.

Special tip

Slightly older children can crawl through holding a glass of water without spilling it, or holding a bat in both hands as they crawl.

And another thing!

With several children playing, time them to see who can complete it the fastest. Get them to beat their own previous best.

Making a toy city

What to do

He can plan and construct a miniature city with milk cartons, cereal boxes, and other cartons. You can also make your own bricks, by mixing earth, flour, and water, molding into tiles and baking them.

Buildings can be made from small boxes, using twigs for log cabins, or from home-made clay bricks. Make a road with sand or mud. Milk cartons are good for buildings with sloping roofs. He can use empty yogurt and similar plastic cartons to adorn the tops of other buildings. Older children can lay out streets, parking areas, and shopping centers on a large piece of cardboard.

How it helps your child to learn

Improves creativity and spatial-visual ability.

Special tip

Complete with toy cars and trucks, Lego models, grass cut from green felt, trees from twigs, and shrubs from cotton wool dipped in dye.

And another thing!

You can use home-made bricks to make bridges, walls, garages, dams. or even The Great Wall of China!

Visual thinking

What to do

Encourage your child to draw simple maps of a treasure island, the garden, etc. Another way is by converting doodles into drawings. For example:

A dot • can be converted into an eye  a bull's eye 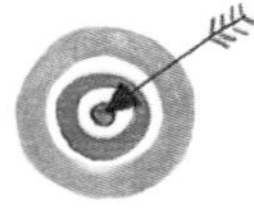 what else?

A square can be converted into a house a box  what else?

An oval  can be converted into a spoon 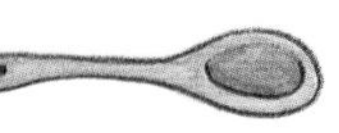 a mouse  what else?

How it helps your child to learn

Using pictures, images, and diagrams is a major help in solving problems in later life.

Special tip

Always have plenty of paper and colored pencils to hand. Make this a regular game on your kitchen blackboard.

And another thing!

Simply draw a shape, like a circle, and ask your child how many things he can turn it into, for example, the Sun or a flower.

Your own garden theater

What to do

Garden plays and concerts are great fun, especially when friends are around. The youngsters can make up their own plots, costumes out of old clothes, and erect a theater from sheets on a clothes line. They will also love to perform songs and poetry, and get the adults to join in.

How it helps your child to learn

This encourages creativity, plus confidence in public speaking and performances.

Special tip

Don't suggest a theme unless you are asked. Even small children can generally come up with really creative concepts.

And another thing!

Be prepared to give undivided attention to the final play, concert, or magic show when it is performed!

Thinking Skills

"Children are travelers in an unknown land—and we are their guides."

Robert Fisher

Thinking Skills

It's surprising, but the skill of thinking logically to solve problems or to make good decisions is rarely taught in schools. Yet what skill could be more important? You are your child's best chance to grow up as both a logical and creative thinker. You will, however, need to guide him consciously.

Explain aloud how you are solving problems

In adult life, of course, most thinking goes on silently in your head. So it's important that you remember to talk through the decisions you make aloud so that he has a model to follow. As with other things, children learn by watching, listening, and imitating.

In the same way, encourage him to talk out loud about how he is going to solve a problem.

The cards that follow will give you plenty of ideas, but if you want to develop a "thinking" home that encourages tackling problems make sure you:

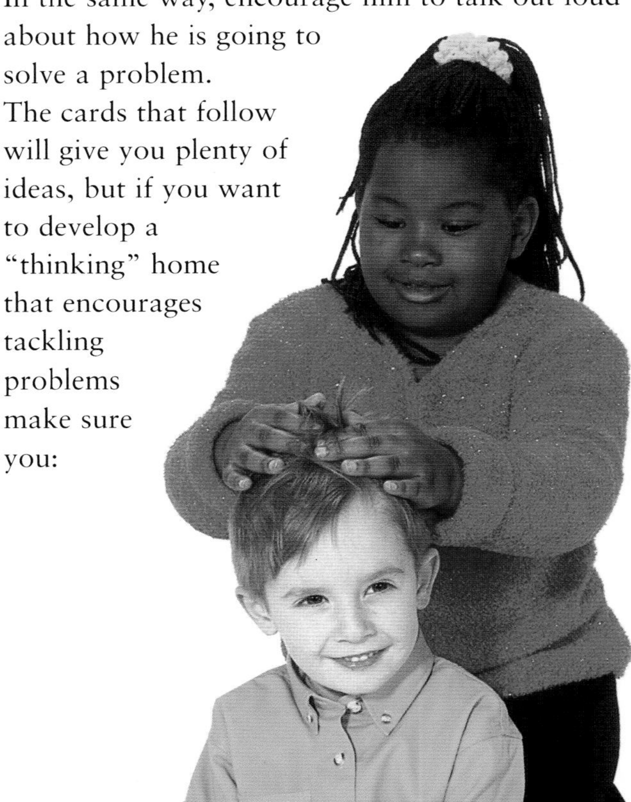

Ponder a lot

- Frequently use phrases like, "What if we did this?" or, "Suppose we tried that?" Good thinkers ponder a lot!
- Ask "Why?" frequently. "Why doesn't the Earth fall down if it's so heavy?" "Why are Daddy's eyes blue and yours are brown?" (Don't worry if you don't know an answer—it's good for him to see you looking things up.)
- Visit museums and examine not just the inventions, but speculate what life would have been like without them. Talk about the lives of inventors like Alexander Graham Bell and Thomas Edison and the persistence that was the key to their success.
- Speculate on things like, "Do animals think?" "How do we know?" "How could you weigh an elephant?" "How does a magnet pick things up?" "How does a flower grow?" "Why do we need to eat three times a day?" "How do they make cornflakes?" "How does the water get into our faucets?"

Invite her to think for herself

If she asks you a question, first ask your child, "What do you think?" It's thinking that develops thinking. Let her figure things out for herself. If you always supply the answer when she asks, she comes to see problems as things that other people can answer, rather than relying first on herself.

Encourage questions

When a child asks a question, praise it, "That was a good question. I like it when you ask questions."

Encourage her to form judgments and justify opinions:

"Was that a good film?" "Was it better than the previous one we watched?" "In what way?" "Is the wolf in *The Three Little Pigs* bad, or just behaving the way that wolves do?"

Involve your child in family decisions. Encourage her, too, to make reasoned arguments for what she believes in.

Make TV an inter-active experience

When she's watched a program, ask questions like, "What was the story about?" "Why do you think the character behaved like that?" "How else could the story have ended?" "Shall we find out more about...?" In other words, switch the brain on when the TV is switched off! And remember that by the time she has left school, she will have watched an average of 22,000 hours of TV versus 11,000 hours of being in school.

The problem with too much TV is that its language is oversimplified and rarely builds vocabulary. It is also passive, requiring little thinking, and research indicates it may be reducing children's attention spans.

Encourage collections

When a child makes a collection—of stones, shells, leaves, or anything—she develops observational skills. She also starts to think about differences and similarities and putting things in groups.

Encourage her to see other points of view

Children naturally see themselves as the center of the world. It's important to encourage them to imagine what it would feel like to be someone or something else. For example, what would it be like to:

- Live in an igloo or a desert tent?
- Be a bus driver, an artist, or a sailor?
- Have no food or shelter?
- How would Cinderella have felt when her sisters went to the ball?

Play mind games

Play lots of games that use mental imagery. Almost half the brain's capacity is taken up in processing visual images.

The more you help your child picture things in her mind, the better she will be able to remember information in later life. So ask her to picture and describe her toys as you drive along—or Grandma's front door, or what you had for lunch yesterday.

Encourage lots of ideas

When you are playing a game that calls for an indeterminate number of answers, like "How many types of birds can we think of?" Don't settle for the obvious. Keep going and you'll find that you'll eventually get to sea birds and from there to albatross, puffin, cormorant as well as the more obvious seagull.

Creative people don't necessarily have better ideas than others, but they usually have more ideas.

Use the dictionary and encyclopedia a lot. Show her that she can answer her own questions. Use reminders and check lists so she sees the value of being systematic.

Set goals

Set out goals and break them down into small, achieveable chunks, so she sees how to plan.

How does a leopard roar?

Can you dance like a ballerina?

What's wrong with your bunny?

I'm thinking of...

What to do

Think of an object and give its definition e.g., "I'm thinking of an animal that hops and lives in ponds." (frog) You can also announce what letter the object begins with, e.g., "I'm thinking of a word that means frozen rain and begins with 's'." (snow)

"I'm thinking of an animal that flies, hangs upside-down, and lives in caves." (bat)

How it helps your child to learn

Encourages your child to be deductive, and to classify thinking in concepts.

Special tip

Start simple so she gets the idea, then extend the idea to body parts, food, furniture, rooms, etc.

And another thing!

There's almost no limit to this game. You can think of characters in stories, people she knows, famous people, or local landmarks.

Predicting

What to do

Encourage your children to predict what is going to happen. What is the logical next step? "The weather today will be cold. So what do you think you should wear?" "That smells good. What do you think we're having for tea?" "Grandma's coming for dinner, so how many places do we need to set?" "How do you think this video is going to end?"

Look for pictures in a magazine (or story book.) Ask, "What do you think happened before this. What do you think will happen afterward?"

How it helps your child to learn

Encourages your child to start taking control over his thoughts.

Special tip

Try simple "if" questions: "If the movie starts at two and it takes us an hour to drive there, what time do we need to leave?"

And another thing!

When you're reading a story, pause occasionally and ask your child, "How do you think this is going to end? What will happen next?"

It's a type of...

What to do

Start off by saying, "A potato is a type of... ." Wait for the answer—which would usually be vegetable. If your child answers "food," that's also correct and gives you a chance to discuss and define what a category is. Introduce the game and the idea of category by saying something like, "A rabbit is a type of animal. What is a sparrow?"

How it helps your child to learn

Gets your child to understand categories and logical groupings.

Some ideas to start you off:

skirt . . . . .clothing
airplane . . . . .transportation
pink . . . . .color
beef . . . . .meat
gold . . . . .metal
tennis .game
trumpet . . . . .musical instrument
orange . . . . .fruit or color

Special tip

Alternatively ask, "How many things can you buy in a (pet/stationery/food/meat/shoe/cake/clothes) store?"

And another thing!

Later on, you can try occupations, currencies, countries, furniture, insects, reptiles, plants, etc.

What comes next?

What to do

Place some used match sticks on the floor or a table in the following sequence and ask, "What comes next?"

You can play the same game with lots of number or letter patterns.

12, 23, 34, 45

What's next?

AAA B AAA B AAA B

What's next?

How it helps your child to learn

Develops logical thinking skills.

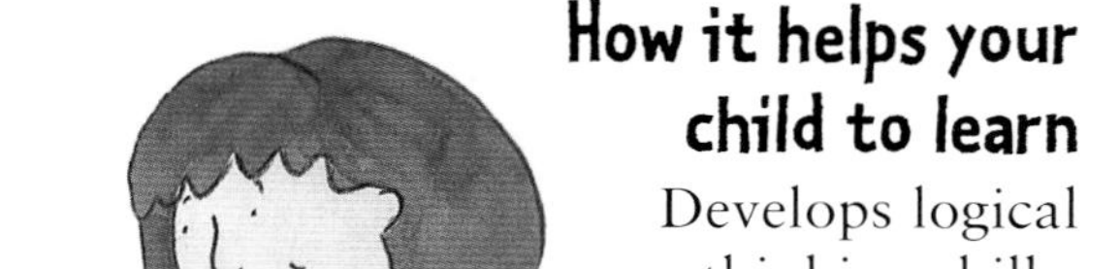

Special tip

For variety, play the game with other items—different sized buttons, colored crayons, playing cards.

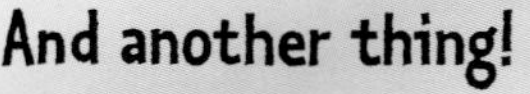

And another thing!

You can also play it with shapes.

Following directions

What to do

Give your child a pen and a piece of paper.
Call out instructions while he draws or writes, e.g.:

a. Draw a square in the middle of the page.
b. Draw a line down the middle of the square.
c. Write an "a" in the left half of the square.
d. Write a "p" in the right half of the square.
e. Draw a circle under the square.
f. Draw a man on top of the square.

How it helps your child to learn

Encourages careful listening and the importance of understanding and following instructions precisely.

Special tip

When you start using this activity, don't bring too many elements in to it or it will confuse your child. Wait until he is more confident.

And another thing!

You can also reverse roles. Allow him to give you a series of instructions which you carry out and then check them with him.

Opposites and pairs

What to do

Simply start by saying, "The opposite of 'white' is 'black.' The opposite of 'tall' is 'short.' What's the opposite of 'woman'?"(man)

Pair words

With this game, you are seeking phrases that always seem to go together, as to the right:

How it helps your child to learn

The game is a good way to introduce prefixes, like **un**- (kind/**un**kind, fair/**un**fair) or **de**- (increase/**de**crease) or **mis**- (understand/**mis**understand.)

Special tip

Use the repeat/bounce combination to learn numbers e.g., 1 plus 1 is 2 (bounce), 2 plus 1 is 3 (bounce), 3 plus 1 is 4 (bounce).

Opposites

quiet/noisy
full/empty
night/day
in/out
work/play
soft/hard
summer/winter
up/down
friend/enemy
old/new
father/mother
deep/shallow

Pairs

cup and (saucer)
needle and (thread)
up and (down)
stop and (go)
night and (day)
bread and (butter)
king and (queen)
pencil and (paper)
soap and (water)
brother and (sister)
husband and (wife)
thunder and (lightning)

Riddle of the day

What to do

Give your child a "logical riddle" each day, "What's white and wet and goes on cornflakes?" or "What purrs and scratches and likes to drink milk?" or "What purrs, scratches, growls, and has cubs?" In each case, take him through his answer to see if it fits all the clues. So while a cat fits the second riddle, a lion or a tiger fits the third. Start simply. Encourage your child to visualize the riddle and ask him to explain why he chose the answer he did.

Some sample riddles

"I can travel under water. I am not a fish. My name starts with an S. I carry people." A good answer is a submarine, and a riddle posed in this way encourages youngsters not to jump to conclusions, but to think logically.

"Most houses are built with me. I'm usually red. I end in 'ck'." (brick)

"I stand still by the side of the road. I change color often. I stop cars." (traffic lights)

"I've got two sleeves. You wear me often. I'm sometimes made out of wool." (sweater)

"I'm the opposite of heavy. Also of dark. I rhyme with bite." (light)

"I'm an action word that starts with 'c'. You do this if someone throws a ball to you." (catch)

"I start with 's'. I end in 's'. People walk up me to go to bed." (stairs)

"You can't see me. But you can feel me when I blow. I start with 'w'." (wind)

"I get wetter as you get dry. I begin with a 't' and end in 'l' ." (towel)

"All plants need me. I begin with 'r'. I end in 'n'." (rain)

"I go to sleep all winter and when I wake up I like honey. I rhyme with share." (bear)

"I start with a 'p' and you can write with me." (pen or pencil)

Note: Vary the mix of clues, sometimes use rhymes, other times give a starting letter, or a finishing letter, etc.

How it helps your child to learn

This encourages logical and deductive thinking, and builds vocabulary.

Special tip

Try rhyming riddles, too. "I have a trunk and rhyme with 'ant.' Who am I?" "I say oink, oink, and rhyme with 'twig.' Who am I?"

And another thing!

You can turn the riddle into a "What am I?" game by rephrasing it, "I purr when I am happy. I scratch when I am cross..."

Odd one out

What to do

Make up groups of four words, where one doesn't fit, such as sparrow, owl, seagull, rabbit. Either write them down or say them to your child. Tell him three are similar, one is different—which one? If he doesn't spot the difference, go through the reasons: "Sparrow: that's a bird… Rabbit: that's an animal." Then go straight on to another example.

How it helps your child to learn

Evaluation and judgment often rely upon the ability to see similarities and differences in situations.

Special tip

Always explain how you and your child come to the answer. In this way, he learns the process of logical thought.

Some categories to use

Trumpet, violin, screwdriver, drum.
Walk, run, hop, think.
Hat, coat, gloves, underpants.

Horse, cow, ant, pig.
Boat, ship, train, canoe.
Fish, crab, bird, shark.
House, car, igloo, castle.
Policeman, teacher, firefighter, blackboard.
1, 3, 5, 4.

The Planet of Id

What to do

Explain that this game is about a new planet called Id.

It has all sorts of funny creatures on it. First there are the Ocks (draw 3 simple creatures with horns.) But there are other creatures that are not Ocks. Draw 3 more simple creatures without horns—but don't say what the difference is. Now draw six

more creatures, some with horns, some without horns. Then ask whether your child can point out which are Ocks from the new drawings. Other creatures you could draw: 4 legs versus 2 legs; noses versus no noses; tails versus no tails.

How it helps your child to learn

The ability to see common characteristics and draw conclusions is key to systematic analytical thought.

Special tip

Guide her through the process step by step, telling her to look for differences and similarities.

And another thing!

When you're reading or talking, take care to talk about **characteristics**—for example, all mammals feed their young with milk.

Is it a fact or opinion?

What to do

Start by explaining to your child the difference between fact (what is generally and objectively considered to be a true statement) and opinion (what is a personal belief, but may not be true.)

For instance:
Rain always falls downward from the sky—FACT.
It is going to rain tomorrow—OPINION.

Then, have fun developing your own Fact v Opinion statements.

Fact—I love *Art Attack*. Opinion—*Art Attack* is the best TV program.

Special tip

You can use a similar idea to ensure he understands "the truth" versus "a lie", or true or false.

How it helps your child to learn

Makes him aware of the difference between fact and opinion in a real-life way.

Fact	Opinion
A fly is an insect.	A fly is the dirtiest insect.
Dogs have four legs.	Dogs make the best pets.
Ice-cream is cold.	Ice-cream is the best treat.
We get milk from cows.	Milk tastes better than orange juice.
London is the capital of England.	London is more fun than Paris.
Football is a very popular sport.	Football is more exciting than basketball.

Order, order

What to do

Think of four things that can be put in order e.g., height, weight, steps in a process, age, etc.
Then ask your child to work out the order—you will have muddled them up first.

Special tip

Start with simpler concepts like age or size.

Some ideas to start you off:

Adult, baby, child, teenager (age)
Hundred, ten, five, thousand (numbers)
Cat, mouse, giraffe, donkey (size)
Wheat, bread, dough, flour (stages)
Oak tree, timber, acorn, furniture (stages)
Pebble, sand, rock, mountain (size)
Week, hour, day, year (length of time)
kennel, garage, house, castle (size)

And another thing!

Later you can explore much more complex ideas, like the value of things, or even population sizes.

Music

"Music is the interstate highway of the memory system."

Terry Wyler Webb and Douglas Webb in **Accelerated Learning with Music.**

Music

Of all the languages a child could learn in life, probably none is as universal as music.

If your child is exposed to a wide variety of music from an early age—including the Baroque, classical, and romantic eras—and to singing from a wide variety of cultures, she has the best chance of developing a good level of musical intelligence. The ability to develop listening skills is also a key part of learning, and both listening and musical abilities are closely linked with the development of a child's brain. Life is a process of organizing and interpreting patterns. It starts with the patterning of movement. And very early on, from about five months before birth, the emerging brain starts to pattern its ability to process sound. The hearing system is virtually complete by four months after birth. Movement and rhythm stimulate an infant's frontal lobes, which are the parts of the brain that will enable it to think and speak. Those frontal lobes grow massively in the first six years of life. So stimulating the frontal lobes during these years will lay down a solid foundation for pattern recognition and fluent speech. That's why researchers have detected a connection between musical skill and mathematical skill.

They both involve the interpretation of patterns. The same area of the brain is active when a human is reading music or playing a musical instrument, as when he is working on a mathematical problem.

Introducing music

There are several activity cards to develop musical skills—here are some more ideas.

Scales—Sing the tonic sol-fa scale together i.e.: doh, ray, me, fa, so, la, te, do.

Rest—Play some music and freeze whenever there is a rest to emphasize that periods of quiet are a part of music.

Recognizing tunes—Hum a song she knows, or sing "la, la" instead of the words. Can she recognize it? Now stop when you get to a particular word. Can she guess what it is? Reverse the roles—let her stop and challenge you.

How many ways?—Take a short, simple song. How many ways can you sing it? Softly, loudly, fast, slow, in a whisper, high, low. Can you hum it, clap out the rhythm, or stamp the rhythm?

Rhythm—Beat out a rhythm on your steering wheel—can she copy it?

Ask your librarian—Your local library has lots of music for children from many different countries.

Listening/action songs

A listening song

"There was a farmer who had a dog and Bingo was his name, oh B–I–N–G–O, B–I–N–G–O, B–I–N–G–O, Bingo was his name, oh."

The first time, sing all the words and all the letters.

The 2nd time, drop the last letter "O," and let her sing it.

The 3rd time, drop the "G" and "O," and let her sing them.

And so on until she's spelling the entire word. Vary it with any animal—a cat, duck, or with any five-letter name, like Peter or Sally.

How it helps your child to learn

Helps listening skills and is a wonderful reading and spelling game if coupled with a blackboard.

Action songs

Sing this song to the tune of John Brown's Body.

"John Brown's daughter had a cut upon her knee (repeat 3 times.)

So he cuddled her and took her out to tea."

1st time, sing the song without actions.

2nd time, substitute a mimed pat on the head for "daughter."

3rd time, mime the word "cut."

4th time, substitute touching your knee for the word "knee."

5th time, mime "cuddled."

6th time, mime drinking a cup of tea.

Home-made music

What to do

Fill salt shakers or empty small glass jars with a variety of substances that can make a noise: sand, rice, seeds, shells, raisins, or dried peas. Fill two containers with each substance. Get your child to close her eyes, shake each jar and find those that match. Then get her to select the loudest, working down to the one that makes the least noise. If you have some Calypso, Latin American music or other fast-moving music, get her to shake out the rhythm.

How it helps your child to learn

Teaches good auditory discrimination.

Special tip

Elastic bands stretched over cartons make good guitars. Bottles can make a xylophone and tin cans make drums.

And another thing!

With several children present, use the jar-shaking technique to make up a band—with home-made drums and bottle xylophones.

Listening skills

What to do

The silence game: Sit or stand still (indoors or out) and ask him to identify all the sounds he can hear. You can also tape-record sounds on a nature walk and replay them later.

Summarize: Now and again, when you are talking to him, stop and ask him to repeat what you said.

Identifying instruments: Ask him to identify musical instruments as you are listening to music. *Peter and the Wolf* and Disney's *Fantasia* are ideal for this.

VROOM

How it helps your child to learn

Being able to listen well is a vital school-age skill.

Special tip

Suggest that he tries to copy the sound of a blackbird, a ringing telephone, a gurgling stream, or a growling tiger.

And another thing!

See how low you can whisper and still be heard—get him to do the same.

Moving to music

What to do

Once a child knows how to walk and run, do dance exercises together to music. Encourage her to move her body in a variety of ways: balancing, swaying, turning, stretching, and bending, and show her how to dance fast and slow, march, and move to show happiness and sadness.

Vary this by dancing in front of the mirror. Explain terms like sway, jig, hop, wiggle, and march.

How it helps your child to learn

This helps develop musical ability and vocabulary, stimulates muscle development and aids muscle memory. It's also a good start to learning by movement.

Special tip

Try a variety of different musics to move to: ballet, classical, jazz, rock, blues, or any of your family's favorite types.

And another thing!

Take turns to improvise arm and leg movements for each other to follow—like a dance routine.

Draw to music

What to do

Arrange for your child to have some blank paper and different-colored markers. Suggest she listens to music and moves the pen the way the music "tells her." Stress that the idea is not to draw a picture, but to create whatever patterns the music suggests to her. Encourage her to "let herself go" and get into the mood of the music.

How it helps your child to learn

Drawing to music helps your child appreciate the emotion conveyed by music.

Special tip

Show how to connect music to emotions, for example, "This bit makes me feel all yellow, wiggly, and happy. This bit is more sad and feels sort of dark blue. How does it make you feel?"

And another thing!

You can draw your own version of how it feels at the same time and compare results. Try the music from the next activity.

Music selections

What to do

You can borrow a wide selection of music from your public library. This card suggests some ideas.

How it helps your child to learn

Most cultures pass on their traditions and beliefs in song and dance. The more your children learn the same way, the more they come to appreciate the differences and similarities that enrich life.

Special tip

When you invite your child to join you in listening to some music, ask her to tell you what it makes her think about.

Evocative music selections

The William Tell Overture—*The Flight of the Bumble-bee* *Swan Lake* —Dvorak's *Largo*—Handel's *Water Music*—Vivaldi's *The Four Seasons*—Beethoven's *Pastoral Symphony*—Beethoven's *Emperor Concerto*—*2001 Space Odyssey*—Chopin's *Piano Concertos*—Mozart's *Eine Kleine Nachtmusik*—*Chariots of Fire*.

Music from other countries

International: The Dietrichson Global Village—music from around the world.

Europe: Selections from the great composers—Bach, Beethoven, Brahms, Chopin, Handel, Haydn, Mendelssohn, Mozart, Prokofiev, Schubert, Tchaikovsky.

Opera: Tapes and video from "The Three Tenors"—Pavarotti, Domingo, and Carreras.

Dancing: Strauss's waltzes, Gershwin's *American in Paris*.

Relaxation: *Watermark* by Enya and *Deep Breakfast* by Ray Lynch.

Science and Nature

"Children's brains are programmed to see the world around them for patterns of meaning."

Robert Fisher

Science and nature projects

Your 21st century child will be at an advantage if he learns the basics of scientific thinking early. Indeed, all you need to do is provide some thought-provoking ideas, because the essence of science is wondering and experimenting—and children are naturally good at that.

Your child is thinking scientifically when he:

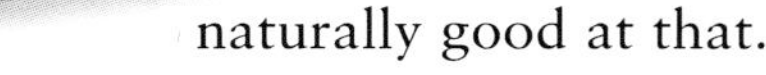

- Becomes good at close observation, seeing small objects and insects, new types of leaves or flowers.
- Becomes good at comparing and classifying—sees the similarities and differences between, for example, ants, spiders, wood lice, or different types of flowers.
- Does experiments to see, for example, why things float or which objects magnets pick up.
- Wonders how things work and (with your permission!) takes them apart or asks to see them demonstrated.
- Sustains a long-term interest in a particular subject like farming, dinosaurs, weather, or birds.

It's worth looking back at that list again. How can you foster those interests? Probably the most important thing you can do is to constantly wonder aloud and experiment for yourself.

"Let's look at it through the magnifying glass." "Let's feel it (taste it/sniff it/look at it.)" Science is always asking questions—questions that mostly start with: "I wonder why..." or, "I wonder how..." then finding out through thinking. Here are some specific ideas to spark others of your own.

Science Projects

- I wonder if we could grow seeds in just water? Do they need earth?
- How does a faucet work?
- When the kettle boils, where does the steam go? (look at the window for a clue.)
- If we breathe on a mirror, we get steam. Does this mean we have water inside us?
- Does the Sun always rise in the same part of the sky?
- Do all bees look alike? How do they find their way back to their hive?
- Which will float —a hair clip or a cork? Is it the size that makes things float?
- What happens to the gas we put into the car?

Young scientists need an enquiring mind and an urge to explain things.

Invest in Scientific Magic

A good magnifying glass and magnet make two of the best toys for your child.
Let her examine her fingernails, hair, and skin pores with the glass. Take each member of the family's fingerprints and let her see the difference. Try leaves, wood, or insects, too.
Examine the parts of a flower: the pistil, stamen, and ovary. Show her how you use a reference book to check what they are.
Experiment with the magnet. What does it attract? Why? Why not other things?

How it helps you child to learn

The basis of science is curiosity. Put a steel screw on top of a card and the magnet underneath. Can you make it move? Can you make a game out of this idea?

Special tip

List things that are magnetic and non-magnetic on paper. This is basic classifying.

And another thing!

If your child shows interest, consider investing in a microscope and taking samples from ponds and earth.

Getting into nature

What to do

Encourage your child to enjoy nature. Not just on long walks and days spent in the garden, but all the time. Help him to collect things from the garden, such as twigs, snail shells, odd-shaped pebbles, and different leaves.

Even encourage an interest in insects, but if your child wants to look at them, don't let him harm them. Look but don't touch. Get him to draw what he sees and color it in.

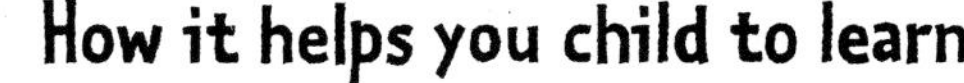

How it helps you child to learn

The essence of science is to experiment creatively. This activity should stimulate your child's interest in the world around him.

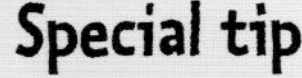

Special tip

A magnifying glass or microscope reveals even more of the micro-world of wood lice or centipedes under bark and leaf mold.

And another thing!

If a child shows great interest in any of these activities, consider investing in a good science kit.

Making structures

What to do

Provide some wire, pliers, and modelling clay. Explain to your child that she can cut the wire into different lengths to design and build a structure. She could even plan or sketch a design in advance.

Explore issues with her such as how to make the construction stronger, or how to build a bridge. Could she make a skyscraper? How about covering the outside with paper?

How could we test the strength of it? With weights? What causes it to balance or overbalance?

How it helps your child to learn

She's building hand-eye coordination, logic, and visual-spatial intelligence.

Special tip

Instead of wire which needs to be cut, you could provide paper-clips which need to be straightened out using the pliers.

And another thing!

If you don't think your child is ready for pliers and wire, try pipe cleaners, tooth picks, or plastic straws.

Exploring butterflies

What to do

- When you go on walks in the country, or in the garden, or park, see if you can find some caterpillars. Explain that this is what a butterfly looks like when it is young. Read a book showing the life cycle of a butterfly.
- Draw two or three large outlines of butterflies. Get your child to cut up some multi-colored tissue paper and paste it on to the wings. Then sprinkle some water on the paper to make it crinkle.
- Ask your child to stand on white paper, her feet a few inches apart. Trace around both feet. Then draw an oval body and two antennae. Get her to color it in.

How it helps your child to learn

It combines nature study and visual art.

Special tip

For butterfly stories, try *The Very Hungry Caterpillar* by Eric Carle and *The Butterfly's Ball* by William Roscoe.

And another thing!

Butterflies are also good starting points for discussing ecology with older children.

Experiments with plants

What to do

Try growing various plants indoors and turning them into nature-study experiments. Start by planting one bean in a small amount of soil in six plastic cups. Water the bean in cup 1 once a day, in cup 2 twice a day, and in cup 3 once a week. Put cup 4 in the dark, cup 5 in sunlight, and cup 6 in the fridge. Water cups 4, 5, and 6 equally regularly. Make sure your child keeps a notebook, or sticks in some markers to record what has been done to each seed.

How it helps your child to learn

This demonstrates the elements that are needed for growth. Better still, she should predict what will happen.

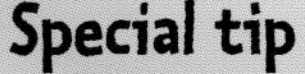

Special tip

As a variation, use sawdust instead of soil in a glass jar. Water your plants regularly, watch what happens—and record it.

And another thing!

When you take an "eye" from a potato or slice the top from a carrot or parsnip, put the cut section in a shallow dish with some water.

Nature "I spy"

What to do

Go on nature trails, but decide beforehand what you both expect to see. Write the items down on a clipboard. The game is to check off as many predictions as possible.For example, she might predict she'll see an oak tree, fir cone, snail, beetle, butterfly, blue flower, or a blackbird, but then find that she sees a spider's web as well.

How it helps your child to learn

This encourages reading, concentration, making predictions, and methodical observation. It is much more involving than a simple walk.

Special tip

Don't forget to include clouds—they give the opportunity to explain the difference between the various types. Borrow or buy a book to help you explore the skies more thoroughly.

And another thing!

Play animal detectives. Look for tracks, nests, gnawed bark (chewed by rabbits/deer,) and broken snail shells (broken by thrushes.)

How does the body work?

What to do

Create a life-size outline of her on some old wallpaper. Mark in features like joints. Discuss how the knuckles, elbows, knees, and waist fold.

Look in an encyclopedia and draw in some bones, as well as the main organs—heart, lungs, liver, and stomach. Teach her how to take her pulse.

Tape her thumb and first finger together and ask her to pick something up. Discuss how humans have fingers and thumbs opposite each other and this makes us good at making things. Contrast that with paws and hooves.

How it helps your child to learn

Children learn best by doing first and then discussing their conclusions afterward.

Special tip

Get her to try crossing the room with her eyes shut or with oil smeared on sunglasses. What does she think it's like to be visually impaired or blind?

And another thing!

Cover her ears. What does she think it's like to be deaf? Discuss a bit about sign language.

Water experiments

What to do

Take a funnel, and see how long it takes for a bottle of water to flow through it. How could you slow it down? With a marble? With cotton wool?

Which of a group of objects float or sink? Use a chart to predict and record your results. Can floaters hold up sinkers?

What dissolves in water? Try sand, sugar, salt, oil, flour, paper, coffee, and jam.

Put some red or blue food dye into a jug of water and then put a cut stick of celery or a carnation into the jug. Will the dye creep up the stalk? Ask her to predict. Why does water rise up a stem?

On a hot day, go out with a bucket of water and a paint brush. Paint a picture with the water. Where does the water go? Use it to tell her how water evaporates to form clouds that later fall to Earth again as rain.

How it helps your child to learn

Look for every chance to create experiments— using different ingredients for milk shakes, trying new recipes, and finding new ways to play with toys.

Special tip

What happens to ingredients when you heat the water or use a whisk? Does more dissolve? Why?

And another thing!

Where does steam from the kettle go? Breathe on a mirror—does the steam mean we have water inside us?

"We are what we repeatedly do.
Excellence, then, is not an act but a habit."

Aristotle.

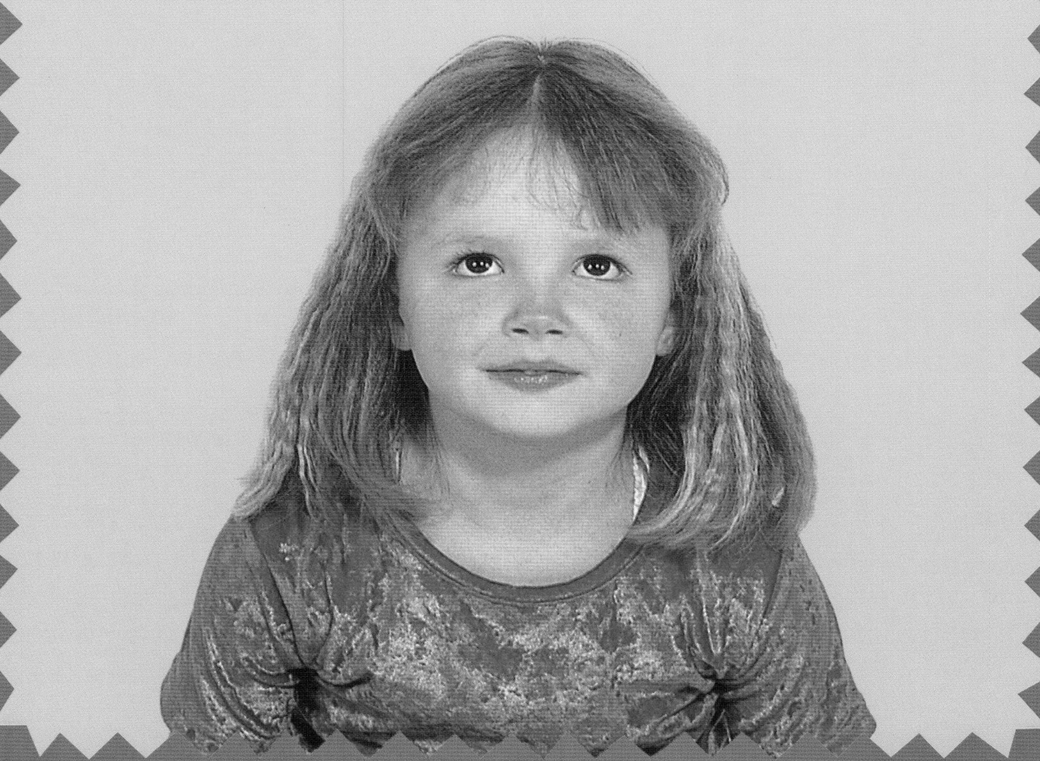

Memory and concentration

The ability to store and recall information can be greatly aided by simple tips learned early in life. A good memory is a vital building block for success.

Here is a guide to developing a good memory.

We remember things more easily if they are associated with something we already know.

The brain appears to organize itself by linking. So when we think of cats, we also link that word to other cat associated words like lion, tiger, lynx, paws, whiskers, stalking, feline, etc.

Get your child used to seeing the connection between things. Many of the Activity Cards will help with that.

The brain stores information best when that information is linked to several senses.

We can remember a Golden Delicious apple more easily if we can see it, smell it, touch it, taste it, and eat it, while someone tells us its name and a little of its history.

Concentrate to remember

Get your child used to looking hard and making strong mental pictures of what he's trying to remember. For example, imagining objects balanced on top of each other will help his memory later.

We remember well when we're emotionally involved.

Almost everyone can remember the pleasant atmosphere of a family kitchen from early in life. In scientific terms, that is because the emotional center of the brain is situated very close to the part of the brain that helps transfer information to long-term memory.

That's why reading together cuddled up in bed builds positive associations with reading. And why it helps to make up a story to remember a group of words. So teach him, for example, to make up amusing stories to remember a word list.

Combining words and music aids memory

It is easier to remember the words of a song if you also hear the tune.

That's because the ability of the right brain hemisphere to evaluate rhythm and music is linked to the ability of the left brain to process words. This is why poetry and nursery rhymes are easy to remember, and why we can remember the number of days in each month through the rhyme which begins, "Thirty days has September…"

So teach your child the use of rhythm and rhymes, chants, and jingles to remember things like a phone number or the days of the week.

Register it to remember it

Two of the keys here are attention and repetition. Teaching your child to really concentrate and look hard is the first step in building a good memory. The Cup Game and other games encourage that.

The subconscious mind is important

Scientists who scan people's brains tell us that, in the period between full consciousness and sleep each night, our brain switches to a different wavelength. They call that stage REM sleep (from Rapid Eye Movement.) It's almost as if part of your brain is "running a movie" of the main events of the day, ready to add them to the brain's "memory banks."

If you can learn to relax just before you go to bed, and start thinking about the main lessons of the day, you will help that storage process. That's why it's preferable for a young child to "wind down" at the end of the day, and to talk softly to him about the interesting things that have happened —in a relaxed way—so the subconscious can take over the "sorting" process.

Kim's games

What to do

Put five objects on a tray. Let your child study them for a minute or two, then cover the tray. How many items can he remember?

Variation: He studies a number of objects on the tray. Then you put the tray out of sight and remove one item. He must guess which object it was.

Suggested types of objects: Pencils and pens, kitchen tools, numbers, alphabet letters, small ornaments, small toys, playing cards.

How it helps your child to learn

Encourages visual memory—an important way to recall accurately.

Special tip

You can make the game easier or more difficult by varying the number of items that your child has to see and remember.

And another thing!

Suggest he counts the objects first—it's a simple but effective memory strategy. And that he groups objects into categories.

Remembering actions/phrases

What to do

Version 1: Say you are going to do two things and he must watch carefully. For example, you might first touch your ear, and then your nose. Then, when you say "go," he should copy you. When he can master two actions, add a third, and then a fourth.

Version 2: Touch two or more objects in sequence, and have him copy you after a five second delay.

How it helps your child to learn

Point out that it's easier to remember things that are silly, or funny, or unusual, rather than phrases that are ordinary. He's beginning to learn what's memorable.

Phrase of the day

At breakfast agree on a word or phrase to remember for the day. Use phrases that build vocabulary e.g., "Seven emerald green frogs leaping on lilypads." When asked, at any time during the day, he has to tell you.

Ask him what the phrase was after 30 minutes, then again at intervals. Increase the number of words and/or the time interval before you ask. Make it fun by inventing an unusual or silly phrase.

Special tip

Try to always ensure success. If he remembers three actions—but not four—play the game again using only three.

And another thing!

Tell him to do three things—just use words, don't show him. Say it's easier if he repeats the instructions either aloud or in his head.

Memory cards (or Pelmanism)

What to do

From a standard pack of playing cards, take out the sixes, sevens, eights, nines, and tens, shuffle the rest together and deal them face-down on the table in eight rows of four.

Each player turns up two cards to try to make a matching pair. If his pair doesn't match, the cards are turned down again. If they do match, he puts them aside and has another turn. When all cards have been removed, the player with the most pairs is declared the winner.

How it helps your child to learn

An excellent but simple way to encourage concentration and memory training.

Special tip

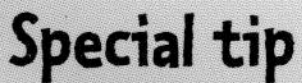

Get the children to name each card turned up, Jack of Diamonds, Queen of Hearts. This will be useful for later card games.

And another thing!

For younger children, use as little as 8 cards. For older children, you can start adding more cards until all 52 are spread out on the table.

Paying attention

What to do

Ask him to look around a room and name everything he sees. Your child will only list a few obvious things at first, so prompt and point out how many things we see, but don't really notice! Do the same thing on a trip to the supermarket.

Get a magazine picture or family photo and let him study it. Now put it out of sight and ask him to tell you everything he can remember about it. Let him study you. Now go out of the room and change something (remove a belt, tie, or earring.) Can he tell what you changed? Then try and ask your child to close his eyes and then say, "What color shirt am I wearing?"

How it helps your child to learn

The essence of concentration is looking hard, and concentration is critical to register something in the memory.

Special tip

Tell him to watch closely as you move a part of your body just a bit. Which part did you move?

And another thing!

When he's recalling pictures you can teach him the value of being systematic—looking from left to right and top to bottom.

Mental hide-and-seek

What to do

The first player visualizes hiding herself, or an object, in a place in the house or garden or anywhere that all the players know well. Then the other players have to guess where she or it is. It helps to learn the "strategy" of asking questions that narrow down the area quickly (as in Twenty Questions.)

How it helps your child to learn

This is an ideal game for car journeys and it also builds visual memory skill—which is a vital learning tool. In fact, this game leads directly to improved spelling—which relies on the ability to make strong mental pictures of the way words look.

Example

Are you in the house ?	yes
Are you upstairs?	yes
Are you in the bathroom?	no
Are you in the bedroom?	yes
Are you on the chair?	no
Are you under the bed?	yes

Special tip

You can also just ask questions that require visual recall—like, "What color is Grandma's car?" or "Where is the bathroom light switch?"

And another thing!

Other questions to develop visual memory: "What did you have for lunch yesterday?" "What side of the bed is your reading light on?"

Memory train

What to do

A simple old favorite to encourage memory and concentration. Imagine you're going on vacation. Start off with the phrase, "I packed my suitcase and put in my... toothbrush."

The game is to repeat the phrase before and add one extra item e.g., "I packed my suitcase and put in my toothbrush and comb." "I packed my suitcase and put in my toothbrush, comb and skirt." And so on.

You can vary it by saying you went into the supermarket and bought groceries, or to the toy store and bought toys.

How it helps your child to learn

Training memory is important for factual learning.

Special tip

Remember to ensure success by starting simply and working up from there.

And another thing!

A similar game is to simply invite your child to recall the sequence of the day at bathtime—or to recall the plot of a video or TV film.

Self-Esteem

"Of all the judgments and beliefs that each one of us owns, none is more important than the ones we have about ourselves."

Wayne W. Dyer in **How to Raise Happy and Healthy Kids.**

Self-esteem

A child's self-image has a big influence on his success at learning or indeed anything else—we tend to become what we think we are.

A child's self-esteem depends overwhelmingly on three interlocking factors:

1. Feeling loved, without reservation, for what he is, not simply for what he accomplishes.
2. Success in achieving goals he sets himself. A feeling of accomplishment. 
3. The positive encouragement he receives—particularly from parents.

All too often children become what others expect. And when parents' negative expectations are telegraphed daily through attitude, words, atmosphere, and body language, then those expectations become the youngsters' limitations.

Your child's self-concept is composed of all the beliefs and attitudes he has about himself. And that self-image conditions him for success or failure.

The following guidelines will help you to build a success-expecting self-image for your child.

A child is not his actions

There's a world of difference between, "You're a bad boy" and, "I love you, but I don't like what you did." The first is a negative label, the second provides reassurance of your basic love and support, but makes clear that you disapprove of the deed. Criticize the action, not the person.

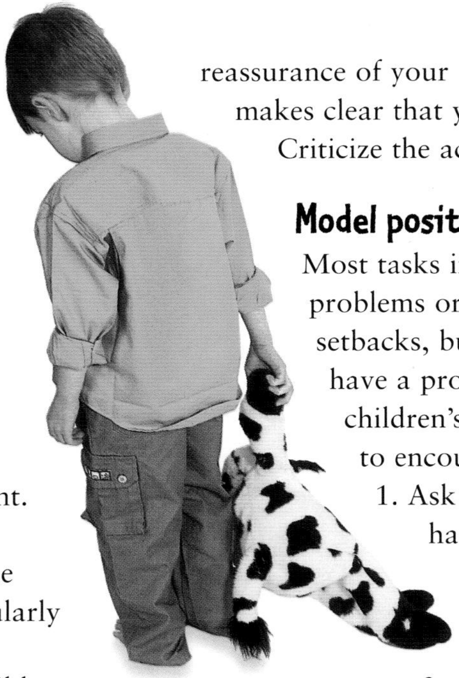

Model positive attitudes

Most tasks in life can be viewed as problems or opportunities. Nobody likes setbacks, but how you react to them will have a profound effect on your children's attitudes. Two simple ways to encourage a positive outlook are:

1. Ask him every day not, "What happened?" but, "What **good** things happened today?" It starts a habit of positive thinking.
2. After a set-back or mistake ask him: "What can we learn from this?" Mistakes that are learned from are part of growth.

A recent study showed that three key elements were common to the families of individuals with high self-esteem:

1. **Each family consistently demonstrated respect, concern, and acceptance**—"love with no strings attached." Each child was accepted for his strengths and abilities, as well as for any limitations and weaknesses.
2. **Each family had clearly defined standards, limits, and expectations**. The children felt secure inside these guidelines.

In other words there were known rules and they were enforced.

3. **Each family operated with a high degree of democracy**. The children were encouraged to participate, to express views, to bring up ideas, even if they differed from the parents.

The simple—but not always easy—principle of discipline: **set the guidelines firmly and don't argue about them—enforce them.** Let her know what is required and insist that she suffers the consequences. In her eyes, arguing or explaining gets the kind of attention she is seeking.

If she breaks the rules, make sure she knows that she is choosing the consequences, for example, being confined to her room for five minutes.

Let your children learn that they are capable—from their own experience. Generally don't rush in to rescue them from their own actions unless those actions place them or others in danger.

Try not to direct them into specific activities. Provide a choice and then encourage participation. Every adult in the future will need to be a self-acting manager, capable of making his or her own decisions. So every child needs to develop that ability early.

Encourage independence. Try not to impose your own goals, or criticize when they are not met. Children get frustrated when adults encourage them to be independent, but then object to their way of doing things. In every activity, your thought should be, "What's the **minimum** help I can give him to ensure he feels successful?"

Expect obedience and you get it. Children tend to do what you expect. If you don't expect them to tidy up—they won't.

Look for every opportunity to reinforce good behavior, rather than nag at bad behavior.

It's vital throughout the growing-up process that children receive tons of positive encouragement. If you need to correct your child, phrase the advice positively so he knows what to do, not what not to do. A **Downer** is negative criticism while an **Upper** is positive criticism. Always try and think before you comment.

DOWNER	UPPER
I hate it when you… (talk so loudly.)	I feel much better when you… (talk to me quietly.)
You always… (leave the towel on the floor.)	I feel so good when you… (pick the towel up.)
You never… (help set the table.)	It's so helpful when you... (set the table.)
I wish you wouldn't…	I like it better when…
Let me do that, you'll only mess it up like you usually do.	Try it yourself and let me know if you want any help.
How many times do I have to tell you—do you ever listen?	You can think for yourself—is that really a good idea?
Why don't you ever think before you speak?	How did you come to think of that?

Notice how the Downer column consists of generalizations which are rarely true and simply cause resentment and defensiveness. In contrast, Uppers help the child know what to do.

The Book of Me

What to do

A child needs to form a clear and positive image of who she is. The Book of Me is a wonderful element in that process. It's a large scrap book recording her early life milestones and achievements.

How it helps your child to learn

Children who feel positive about themselves have higher motivation and are more successful.

Special tip

Review the book and update it regularly—this is a very important activity.

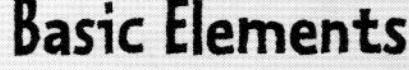

Basic Elements

1. Include name and photo on the cover.
2. Photos of milestones in age sequence.
3. Record of height and weight every 6 months.
4. Favorite cards/postcards.
5. A body picture on wallpaper. Get her to fill in the details from an outline you draw—fingers, nails, hair, facial details.
6. Family handprints and fingerprints.
7. A family tree.
8. Family celebration rituals.
9. Memory map of who she knows.
10. Regular list of what she can do.
11. Portfolio of artwork and photos.
12. Records of her best achievements so far.

All the things she can do

What to do

Sit down occasionally and list all the things that she can already do. Children are faced daily with the things they can't yet do. She needs to realize the progress she is making.

Ask her questions you know she can answer, note what she can do around the house and point out her display of artwork. Explain that everything needs practice before you succeed. Let her try things on her own. Provide the minimum amount of help, yet just enough to nudge your child towards success.

How it helps your child to learn

She will keep trying if she feels good about what she can already do, and about making an effort to do more.

Special tip

Whenever she makes a mistake ask, "What have you learned that will help you next time?" Mistakes are stepping stones towards success.

And another thing!

Get her used to talking about practice rather than mistakes—that's how sports stars view it.

Photographing artwork

What to do

Save your children's models and artwork—but when your refrigerator door gets too crowded with junior masterpieces, take a color photograph of your child in front of the display. Add the photograph to his own portfolio or The Book of Me.

How it helps your child to learn

This serves many purposes: It keeps a record of artistic progress. It creates pride in personal achievement. It shows how big he was as each painting was completed. And assembling the artwork for the best photo is itself a lesson in creativity.

Special tip

With three-dimensional artwork, from home or nursery school, prop your child up on a couch and photograph him with it.

And another thing!

Especially colorful photos, with your child and his parents, could make excellent Christmas greeting cards.

The Effort Coupon

What to do

The Effort Coupon is a powerful idea. When you see your child really trying, even if (or especially if) the attempt is not 100 percent successful, give out an Effort Coupon. Then, when he's collected an agreed number, let him "cash them in" for a treat you share together. It should not be a toy or present, but a visit somewhere together, or some favorite activity together.

How it helps your child to learn

Reinforces the importance of effort and persistence without using a material "bribe."

Special tip

Use stories to emphasize persistence—Robert Bruce and the spider; the 1,000 attempts Thomas Edison made to invent the electric lamp.

And another thing!

Explain how sports stars and TV actors practice over and over again until they succeed. Success requires persistence.

Exploring feelings

What to do

1. Act it out

Suggest he acts out emotions e.g., be angry, sad, happy, afraid, shy, curious, lonely, etc. Then suggest he uses only sounds to express these feelings. How does his body feel when he acts out a different mood?

2. What are they feeling?

Flick through the pages of a magazine. What are the people in it feeling? Use it as a reason to discuss his feelings too. About, for example, his sister or nursery school. Can he draw his feelings?

How it helps your child to learn

A key to self-esteem is to be able to acknowledge and express emotions openly.

Special tip

To encourage him, occasionally tell him how you personally feel and what makes you happy or sad or puts you in different moods.

And another thing!

It's very important he feels it's normal to have feelings so that he doesn't panic when he feels angry or frustrated.

Quiz time

What to do

This is an "anytime" quiz, designed to build up your child's confidence. The wording of the questions should ensure that she always succeeds. So gently prompt for extra responses. Examples:

- Name three things that fall from the sky.
- Name three games that are played with a ball(s).
- Name parts of the body that come in pairs.
- Name three things you put on your head.
- Name three ways to travel.

How it helps your child to learn

By asking her questions she can answer, you build her enjoyment of question-and-answer sessions. This, in turn, boosts her future willingness to take tests.

Special tip

Rich sources of questions: story books, nursery rhymes, animals, cooking, household objects, parts of the body, cars, buildings.

And another thing!

Here are some that are more difficult—name things that ring, clatter, boom, tinkle, buzz, howl, hoot, shine, reflect, and sparkle.

A memory map of who he knows

What to do

Put his name in the middle of a piece of paper. Then branch out with all the people in his life—family and friends, the ones he loves and the ones who love him. As you construct the memory map, point out how remembering one person jogs your memory for others, too.

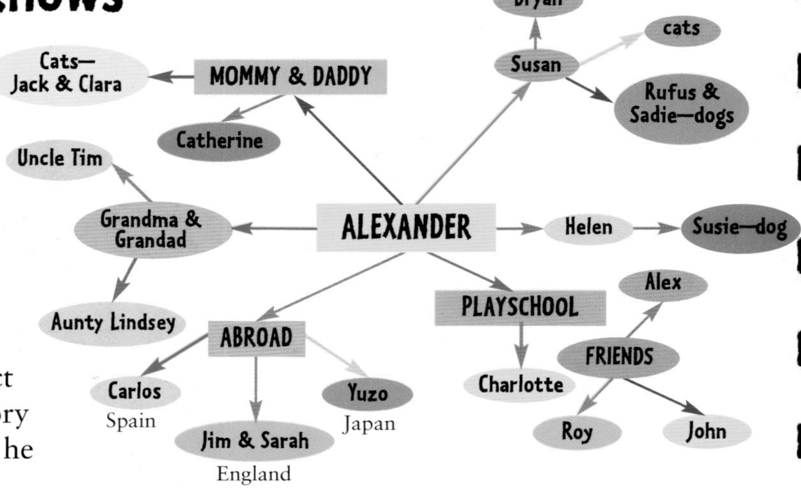

How it helps your child to learn

A very visual way of showing how we all connect and a great introduction to the concept of memory maps or word webs, which will be helpful when he comes to plot stories, or write for school work.

Special tip

Construct the web, but if his writing is good enough, let him fill in the names.

And another thing!

Do a similar word web with one of his friends. He'll see that he is the center of his own world, but that others see the world in a different way.

Loving memories

What to do

As well as physical security, a loving environment is vital for intellectual development.
Although you naturally provide that, here are some less obvious ideas.

- Develop a sign or a family cheer that's exclusive to the family and says you are unique.
- From time to time, invite her to choose something for you to wear.
- Have a surprise award ceremony to mark another achievement.
- Make some bread together, grow a sunflower or a pumpkin—the size is impressive.
- Have a wall space where all her new artwork is exhibited.

How it helps your child to learn

Children that know that they are loved by their parents grow up with an emotional "cushion" around them. The bad times at school or the arguments with friends can all be overcome if they know that when they share the problem with their parents they will recieve unconditional love.

Special tip

Children learn to love by being loved unconditionally. If you provide them with fond memories, they will do the same for their children one day.

And another thing!

It is the unexpected moments of happiness that are most treasured by your child and the ones that stay in the memory.

Values

"The manner in which we listen to the world around us is as individual as our fingerprints."
Don G. Campbell in **Rhythms for Learning.**

Setting Values

We believe that you cannot have high self-esteem without a strong set of values. You also cannot have happiness without a strong set of values, which is why values come close to the top of our Pyramid of Happiness. The only person who can successfully teach your child values is you. Besides, your child will have spent over 40,000 hours of his waking life at home by the time he's eight, versus just 4,000 hours at school!

The initial question is, "What values?". With young children, the rule is always to keep it simple, so we propose you concentrate on just five:

Responsibility—to the home, for yourself.

Self-control—with his temper, his eating, TV-watching, and work.

Respect—politeness, caring, and sharing.

Honesty—telling the truth, playing by the rules.

Courage—doing what is right, even when it's hard.

Making values real to a child

1. Read or tell a story that illustrates the value. Aesop's Fables were created for this purpose! Then discuss the story and emphasize the value that it illustrates.
2. Define the value in simple language and discuss why it's important. Often you can make the point dramatically by showing what happens when people do not follow the value. For example, when people are dishonest, irresponsible, or cowardly.
3. Invent a catchy phrase that sums it up. For example, "We care and we share" sums up most aspects of respect quite neatly.
4. Look for examples in day-to-day life. When you see an example, point it out. It means you must provide a model for the value, too!
5. Reinforce with immediate praise. The secret is to be lavish with praise whenever you see the behavior you seek, and award bonus points.
6. Concentrate on a value a month. Each value should become a "theme of the month." This means that every five or six months, you can go back and reinforce each value. Over the years, that's a lot of positive attention.
7. Promise that you will follow the value and have him make the same promise to you. People make more effort to achieve a publicly-announced commitment. So will your child.

The four principles of teaching values

1. **Emphasize rewards rather than criticism.** Nagging spoils your relationship and doesn't work. Look for every single opportunity to praise and to reward good behavior—or even the beginnings of good behavior!
2. **Explain why each value is important.** It's important that it's the value they obey and not you. That's ultimately the difference between the sort of internal motivation that lasts—and the external motivation that ultimately breaks down.
3. **Your child will learn more from you than from any other person.** Not from what you say, but from how you act. No one is perfect. We all get tired, depressed, overwhelmed, and angry at times. Many of us swear when we shouldn't. But when we do, we send a signal to our children that this is acceptable behavior, because we are doing it. If you do fall below the standards that you want your child to set, apologize, mentioning what you did wrong.
4. **Repeat the values words again and again to emphasize their importance.** Constantly use words like responsible, honest, respect, caring, team-work, and courage. And use their opposites to make the differences clear—irresponsible, dishonest, disrespect, and uncaring. Children need to experience the values, have their understandings of the values reinforced, and learn the correct words to use to describe and name the values.

Introducing the Daily List

On the next page you will see the Daily List. This is a list that tells your child what he is expected to do each day. It is the key to reinforcing good values. When you have decided what will be on your list, make a few copies and hang them up in the house.

The Daily List

Here are a few ideas to add to your list. The template for this list is on page 126.

Something special

This can be doing something special for someone else, or a job done over and above the list. It could also be making a specially big effort at something.

The star system

Award a star when five or more points are earned in a day. This is a great extra visual reinforcement.

What about bad results?

Keep the Daily List focused only on rewarding good behavior and responsibility. You already have a way of dealing with bad results, so don't deduct points.

Administering the Daily List

Consistency is critical. He should fill in the chart with you each evening as a ritual that gives you another chance to praise and reinforce good behavior. At the end of the week, the points are totaled and the reward is made as soon as possible.

Rules

What to do

Children need to be directly involved in setting rules and boundaries. Here's how.

- Hold a family conference and make it special.
- Talk about the need for rules e.g., why we need traffic lights or rules for games.
- Discuss the rules the family needs.
- Simplify and write down the rules.
- Vote on them.
- Agree on appropriate results or punishments for breaking the rules.
- Everyone (you, too!) promises to obey the rules.

How it helps your child to learn

Children (like adults) only feel really committed to rules and agreements they have been involved in creating.

Special tip

Suitable topics: bedtimes, TV watching, politeness, clearing up, behavior, obedience.

Responsibility

What to do

1. Tell the story of the three pigs—how the oldest pig worked hardest and was responsible.
2. Discuss the ways in which you are responsible for your child. (Define the word.)
3. Discuss how he can become responsible—put away toys, feed pets, set/clear table, make bed.
4. Agree on a daily "To Do" list (use the template on page 126.)
5. Review progress against the "To Do" list every evening and award ticks and stars. It only takes a minute.

How it helps your child to learn

You get the behavior you reward, not the behavior you nag about.

Special tip

Praise every success every day and award points and a prize each week. Develop a little ritual after each successful day when he has fulfilled his "To Do" list.

And another thing!

Good behavior bonus points are the ideal way to reward (hence reinforce) **all** the other values.

Self-control

What to do

1. Tell a story that illustrates the importance of self-control (for example, The Seven Labors of Hercules.)
2. Discuss why self-control is important in our family. (Define the word.)
3. Discuss how he can exercise self-control e.g., count to 10 when he's angry, do his daily jobs before watching TV, save pocket money.
4. Teach calming strategies.
5. When he exhibits self-control, reinforce it with praise and good behavior bonus points.

How it helps your child to learn

Children need to learn how to postpone short-term pleasure (e.g., watching TV or spending on trivial things) to gain a long-term reward, e.g., school success or a major purchase.

Special tip

Develop a catch phrase to embed the value, for example, "work first, play later."

And another thing!

Establish a "cool box"— place he goes to calm down rather than react angrily or fight.

Respect

What to do

1. Tell a story that helps define respect (for example, Prince Charming.)
2. Discuss the importance of respect (which includes politeness, obedience, taking turns, kindness, and respect for life.)
3. Discuss how he can show respect (that includes apologizing.)
4. Look for every example of respect that is exhibited, praise it generously and award "good behavior" bonus points.

How it helps your child to learn

Children who understand the various aspects of respect will be socially more successful.

Special tip

Develop a catch phrase to reinforce the value of respect, for example, "We care and we share" or, "Think of others."

And another thing!

Emphasize that a sincere apology allows her to start again and avoid punishment (it wipes the slate clean.)

Honesty

What to do

1. Tell a story that helps define honesty and why it's important (for example, The Boy Who Cried Wolf.)
2. Discuss what honesty means for our family (telling the truth, owning up, not cheating, never taking anyone else's property.)
3. Look for every example of honesty she shows, praise it and award good behavior bonus points.

How it helps your child to learn

Honesty is basic to acquiring social skills.

Special tip

Develop a memorable catch phrase to reinforce honesty, such as "Honesty is best."

And another thing!

Play the "Is it a fact or opinion?" game from this book to reinforce the idea that everyone has their own way of being.

Courage

What to do

1. Tell a story that helps define courage.
2. Discuss what courage means in your family—doing what's right even though it's difficult; saying no when you know something is wrong; trying new situations even if you are nervous; speaking to new people; falling off a bike and trying again; persistence.

3. Look for every act of courage, praise it and consider rewarding it with good behavior bonus points.

How it helps your child to learn

Courage, in the sense of being willing to stick to your moral principles and in being persistent, are key attributes for success.

Special tip

Develop a memorable catch phrase, for example, "Courage my brave."

And another thing!

Let him see you persist in getting something right. He copies most of his values from you!

Caring for other people

What to do

If you cushion your child from all the nasty things that go on in the world, she will grow up thinking that her cozy home environment is a typical environment. Ask her why she thinks people may want to live alone, or why people can't afford to eat properly. Don't burden her with other people's worries, but make her aware of what goes on in the world.

How it helps your child to learn

Learning about how other people live gives your child an insight into other lives. This develops compassion and her understanding of society.

Special tip

Talk to your child about how it might feel to live on the streets or to be too poor to be able to have enough to eat.

And another thing!

A child with a sense of compassion is a child who will have strong relationships with people.

The Daily List

JOBS	MON	TUES	WED	THURS	FRI	SAT	SUN
Clearing the table	✓	✓					
Feeding the rabbit	✗	✓					
Making my bed	✓						
*Good behavior bonus							
TOTAL							

TARGET PRIZE: Trip to fair

TOTAL POINTS TARGET

Resource List

Here is a list of recommended books and websites that will support the learning that your child will have experienced with FUNdamentals.

Recommended Books

Books to encourage basic skills

Help Your Child with Maths, BBC Books 1993
Full Esteem Ahead by Diane Loomans, Kramer Press 1994
Teaching Your Children Values by Linda and Richard Eyre, Simon and Schuster 1993
Brain Power for Kids by Lana Israel, Buzan Centres 1996
MegaSkills by Dorothy Rich, Houghton Mifflin 1988
Raising a Delightful Unspoilt Child by Burton L. White, Simon and Schuster 1994

Practical information on learning

Accelerated Learning for the 21st Century by Colin Rose and Malcolm Nicholl, Piatkus 1998
In Their Own Way by Thomas Armstrong, Jeremy Tarcher 1987

Intelligence

The Unschooled Mind by Howard Gardner, Basic Books 1991

Internet Sites

For an idea of the range of internet websites, first try www.100hot.com which gives you a list of the most popular 100 web sites for children—you'll need to pick out the appropriate sites, though.

For general advice, try www.parentsoup.com, and for sites to visit with your child try:

www.funschool.com
www.kidsdomain.com
www.billybear4kids.com
www.gustown.com
www.theideabox.com
www.enchantedlearning.com
www.quia.com
www.kids-space.org—for music especially

Index

Writing templates

First writing template

Press out the circle and use the shape that's a template only after your child has had plenty of other prewriting practice. See your cards for details. When he's ready for more advanced work, place this template on a sheet of plain cardboard or paper.
Provide colored crayons and encourage your child to trace carefully, using the inside edge as a guide.Then get him to fill the shape in vertical lines, and later horizontal ones across the circle that has been drawn. Later, on fresh paper, remove the template after drawing the circle and get him to trace over the circle in freehand.

Second writing template

Use this circle in a similar way to the first template. Show your child how to hold the circle flat on a sheet of paper or cardboard, and trace around it with a crayon or pencil. After drawing several circles on different parts of the paper she might like to paint them in different colors.
By tracing the big circle outlines in this way, she will soon become competent in making all the alphabet letters that use part of a circle, such as c, o, b, d, and g.

Third writing template

Press out the square and use the shape left in the card as a template. Not only does it teach an infant to draw squares, but it builds the ability to write those letters of the alphabet that have down strokes or cross strokes.
When your child has traced and colored-in several squares quite competently, suggest tracing both circles and squares, making a pattern and coloring that in.

Fourth writing template

Show your child how to hold this square on the paper with her non-writing hand, then trace around the outline. Apart from building confidence in drawing straight lines, this is also useful training for the later use of a ruler.
Again, encourage your child to remove this inset after several attempts, and then trace over the square outline in freehand.

Fifth writing template

Use this in a similar way to the other templates. It provides the practice for writing the strokes that make up letters such as k, x, y, and z.

Sixth writing template

This triangular inset should be used very much like the circle and square, tracing around the outside. Show your child how to tilt the triangle at various angles to make different patterns for coloring in with crayon or paint.

Seventh writing template

By tracing inside this template, your child will learn how to write the curves that make up other letters of the alphabet.

Eighth writing template

As well as building confidence in writing curves, this inset, too, can be used with the circle, triangle, and square insets to draw interesting patterns on cardboard for original artwork.

All insets can also be used to trace over material, which can then be cut out with round-nosed scissors for making textured artwork.

about	add	after	all
am	an	and	any
are	as	ask	at
away	be	before	best
big	black	blue	bus
but	by	call	came
can	car	come	cry
day	did	do	don't

down	drink	eat	end
find	fish	five	fly
for	four	funny	get
girl	give	going	good
got	green	had	has
have	he	help	hen
her	here	him	home
hot	house	how	if

in	into	is	it
jump	let	like	look
made	make	man	many
me	must	my	new
no	now	of	old
on	one	or	out
pig	play	please	put
ran	red	ride	sad

said	saw	say	see
she	sit	six	sleep
slow	stop	sun	tell
that	the	them	then
they	this	three	too
two	up	us	walk
was	wide	with	woman
work	yes	you	young

again	along	also	answer
apple	bear	become	below
bird	boat	by	cake
city	cold	cow	cried
dark	doll	door	drive
duck	easy	egg	ever
every	fall	family	far
farm	fast	father	feel

feet	fire	first	food
friend	from	gave	goes
gone	happy	hard	hello
herself	horse	hour	inside
it's	just	keep	king
kitten	knew	know	land
large	last	late	light
lion	little	live	lost

may	milk	miss	mother
Mr.	Mrs.	name	next
night	once	open	orange
other	over	people	pick
place	pretty	puppy	queen
real	really	right	room
seem	shop	side	some
soon	start	store	street

such	table	take	talk
thank	there	thing	think
time	took	town	toy
tree	try	turn	under
use	very	want	wash
way	went	were	what
when	where	while	white
who	why	year	your

above	across	against	almost
always	animal	another	around
basket	beautiful	because	began
behind	being	better	between
birthday	both	bring	brother
chicken	children	clean	close
country	does	done	draw
during	each	early	earth

eight	enough	farmer	field
flower	found	garden	glad
grass	great	grow	happen
hear	heard	high	hold
however	hurt	idea	kind
later	learn	leave	left
letter	long	lunch	might
mind	money	more	morning

move
much
myself
never

next
nine
nothing
often

only
own
paper
part

party
picture
piece
point

problem
question
quickly
reach

river
round
school
self

seven
shall
sheep
should

show
since
sister
small

stay	stick	still	study
sure	teacher	their	these
those	thought	today	train
true	until	upon	video
voice	wait	warm	watch
water	which	window	wish
without	won’t	wood	word
would	write	yellow	young

Phonic Fun Set 1

Half the English language is phonetic: it is spelled very much as it sounds. The sheets in these sets contain simple phonic words, starting with the "short" vowels. Use them to introduce your child to phonics in easy stages. Start with, say, two sets of eight rhyming cards, and play a game of Phonic Snap. Regularly add more cards to the game. Keep a rubber band around unused cards and store them so the full pack stays intact.

Phonic Fun

Use either of the Phonic Fun Sets. Each contains cards that are spelled as they sound. Deal 10 cards face up to each player. The remaining deck of cards is placed face-down between the players, and the top card is turned face-up and placed alongside the deck. The game is to find four cards that rhyme (such as cat, sat, fat, mat.) Each player, in turn, picks up either the card at the top of the pack or the turned up card.

He then places his best rhyming cards in two columns, and discards a card on the turned-up pile. The winner is the first player to get four rhyming cards in one vertical line.

For beginners, start with Phonic Fun Set 1.

Alphabet game

Deal 16 cards to each player, and leave the rest of the pack face down. The winner is the first player to put down eight cards in alphabetical order, starting with the letter "a."

As each card is put down in order, the player can pick up a replacement from the top of the pack.

Variation: players can start with any letter, to suit their hand, and then put down cards alphabetically from there on.

Matching cards

Deal in the same way as the Alphabet Game. But players try to find four cards that start with the same letter. First to do so wins.

Variation: Find four cards ending with the same letter.

cat sat get set hat pat net yet

bat rat bet pet fat mat met wet

bit	fit	hit	kit
pit	sit	slit	spit
cot	dot	got	lot
hot	not	pot	rot
bad	lad	dad	had
mad	pad	sad	but
cut	gut	hut	nut
rut	tut	shut	jut

den	hen	men	open
pen	ten	then	when
wren	an	ban	can
fan	man	pan	ran
tan	van	all	ball
call	fall	hall	stall
tall	wall	small	ate
date	state	gate	late

mate	plate	hate	crate
bell	smell	fell	sell
shell	spell	tell	well
yell	fun	gun	nun
pun	run	bun	spun
stun	sun	ill	bill
fill	hill	mill	kill
pill	till	will	spill

Phonic Fun Set 2

This set introduces some more phonic words. While the first Phonic Fun set covers mainly simple sounds, this one includes many words with double vowels, such as the "ai" in "fail," and blended consonants, such as the "br" in "brave." Use this set in the same way as the first.

But before you press out each card for games, read your child each set of rhyming words with your finger under each one, so he or she can see how the words read from right to left. This will get your child used to the normal flow of reading. Then show each word individually.

hail tail mite write blink pink mink pest

fail sail kite quite drink link sink nest

bail rail bite site ink wink think best

rest	test	went	west
guest	brick	kick	chick
lick	pick	stick	trick
sick	quick	back	crack
hack	sack	pack	track
lack	black	stack	and
band	hand	land	brand
sand	grand	stand	wave

gave	brave	shave	save
cave	crave	grave	slave
main	pain	rain	stain
brain	drain	train	plain
again	grain	strain	bent
cent	dent	sent	rent
tent	went	spent	event
rang	sang	bang	fang

gang	hang	pang	clang
bump	jump	lump	hump
pump	stump	dump	clump
bake	cake	lake	make
snake	take	rake	stake
flake	block	clock	dock
frock	lock	rock	sock
stock	flock	bank	rank

WHO	DOES WHAT
Our family	eats dinner.
The big girls	like to swim.
My friend	loves to play.
My dog	loves bones.
The teacher	helps us read.
The little bird	has its bath.
My brother	likes to dive.

WHO	DOES WHAT
My Dad	drives home.
The lion	is happy.
Pat and Jim	are invited.
The sun	is hot.
Mom and I	go shopping.
The tiger	eats meat.
Our cat	drinks milk.

WHERE OR WHEN

at the table.	on Sundays
in the sea.	up the hill
at our house.	in the sky.
to my party.	for dinner.
every day.	with friends.
in town.	at his stable.
at school.	in summer.

am	ask	be	call	cry
drink	five	girl	green	hen
house	is	made	may	my
pig	ride	see	six	so
sun	them	too	we	you

an	at	before	came	day
drink	eat	fly	got	give
had	her	how	it	make
new	old	play	she	slow
stop	the	then	two	well

about	an	end	fish	for
come	did	here	jump	man
got	has	sad	sit	sun
on	please	will	yes	you
they	best	big	can	

after	are	away	black	but
cry	don't	find	funny	good
he	home	in	like	me
now	or	ran	saw	sleep
that	three	walk	was	work

Math grid 1

Math grid 2

GAME 1

For children learning to count, show them the dot side of the cards from 1 to 3 in sequence, saying: "This is one. Two. Three ..." You can start as young as two, but make it a game. Gradually work up to 10.

GAME 2

Gather together groups of items, such as one comb, two buttons, three spoons. Show the dot cards in sequence, but say: "This says one and this is one comb ..." Start with the numbers from one to three, and work up.

GAME 3

When your child is familiar with dots and objects from 1 to 10, show the cards again in sequence but showing both sides in turn, and saying: "These are five dots, and this is the number 5; these are six dots, and this is the number 6."

GAME 4

Assemble groups of items, such as two cherries, three apples, and four pears. Show the cards in sequence, turning them over and showing what they represent: "These are three dots; this is the number three, and these are three apples."

GAME 5

Deal five dot cards face-up, and the game is to match each dot card with a numeral from the rest of the pack. If in doubt, he can look at the numeral on the back of the dot-card to see what is needed.

GAME 6

Deal five cards, with the numeral side up. Your child has to match the numeral with the correct number of plastic counters, by placing them neatly under each card. When completed, check the dots on each card to confirm accuracy.

GAME 8

Deal two cards dot side up, and ask your child to add them together. If the score is above 10, get him to find two other dot cards that make up the total (for example, 5 + 6 = 11, so find two other dot cards that equal 11.)

GAME 8

Deal each child five cards. Place the rest in one pile, and the instruction cards (plus, minus,) in another. Each child puts down a card, picks up an instruction card and tries to complete a sum from his hand. Replace played cards. Winner is person with most cards played.

1	1	1	1
2	2	2	2
3	3	3	3
4	4	4	4

Stick this sheet 2 back to back with sheet 1 and then tear cards apart.

FUNdamentals

MATH CARDS 2

=	−	−	−
=	+	+	x
●	●	●	●
● ●	● ●	● ●	● ●
● ● ●	● ● ●	● ● ●	● ● ●
● ● ● ●	● ● ● ●	● ● ● ●	● ● ● ●

5	5	5	5
6	6	6	6
7	7	7	7
8	8	8	8
9	9	9	9
10	10	10	10